Serving

Each Other in Love

George L. Earnshaw

SERVING
each other
in LOVE

The Judson Press, valley forge

Contents

Preface

THERE ARE THREE FUNDAMENTAL CHOICES that any person must make—(1) the choice of a life vocation, (2) the choice of a life mate, and (3) the choice of a life philosophy. Hopefully, our convictions about who we are and why we are here and what we should be doing (a life philosophy) will form the keystone which will hold the arch together.

This book is written in the conviction that something better than a fragmented approach to marriage and family living is necessary. For too many people these days, life appears to be a kind of giant cafeteria where they casually move through, picking up various and sundry isolated ideas that seem to make sense at the moment without any disciplined attempt to have an over-all unifying frame of reference.

Consequently thousands of young people drift into an occupation with the pragmatic rationalization that it pays well, or they choose a mate because she is "good looking" or he is "a marvelous football player." When you match this up with the tragic fact that every day the courts in America are open, some two thousand divorces are granted (and hundreds of thousands of children are involved in these each year), you can see the need for illumination.

Nearly two hundred years ago Edward Gibbon completed his monumental classic, *The History of the Decline and Fall of the Roman Empire*. In this he lists five areas of Roman culture which reflect this decline: (1) higher and higher taxes, (2) the insatiable urge for pleasure, (3) the building up of armaments, (4) the decay of religion, faith becoming a mere formality separating the sacred from the secular, and (5) the rapid increase of divorce, which undermines the sanctity of marriage and the home. If history repeats itself, as many historians claim, then we of today must do all we can to strengthen the sacred institution of marriage.

Any intelligent approach to a philosophy of marriage must deal with three important kinds of questions. First, does life have any meaning? If it does, how is this meaning related to the institution of marriage? And where do we as individuals fit into the scheme of things? Self-identity, the desire for acceptance is basic. Second, if marriage does have meaning for the individuals involved, how do we explain the gnawing anxieties that come from imponderables such as suffering and death? Third, how can we intelligently deal with the selfishness and the hostility that are present in each of us and in some cases get out of control, causing personality damage and guilt and sometimes divorce? In other words, what does our faith have to say about the three basic needs in each of us—status, security, and sociability?

As the social scientists consider such questions as these, they seek to analyze the outward expressions of these things in our culture. Using their tools of research and analysis they have come up with a variety of prescriptions for us to ponder. Researchers like Terman, Popenoe, and Kinsey have sought to study the sex habits of men and women in and out of marriage, and, thanks to their dedicated efforts, we know now a great deal more than we once did about what is actually going on in our society. These findings have sociological value and Christians need to make use of them. In this book, however, we are less concerned with sociology than with man's relationship to God and what that means to the institution of marriage.

There are many good books on the practical aspects of sex, finances, raising children, and the many other areas of marriage and the family. This little volume brings together what to me are the important issues with which a couple in love should be concerned as they prepare for wedded life. If it has any particular originality, it is in theological orientation and organization.

I have made every effort to trace accurately the sources of quotations in this book. If there are any errors or omissions in acknowledgments, they should be reported to the publishers, who will correct them in subsequent printings.

I am deeply in debt to many people who have had a share in this book, especially my family who have inadvertently provided me with a testing ground for my convictions. After twenty years of happily married life and counseling with countless couples contemplating the "leap of faith," I humbly submit this little book, only too aware of its many shortcomings and inadequacies but in the hope that God may use these words and bless them.

GEORGE L. EARNSHAW

SYRACUSE, NEW YORK
FEBRUARY, 1967

Let the word of Christ dwell in you richly, as you teach and admonish one another . . . and whatever you do, in word or deed, do everything in the name of the Lord Jesus, giving thanks to God the Father through him (Colossians 3:16-17).

My House

Let me build my house on firm foundations—Let me dig deep into the impervious granite-like substance that we call basic Christian teachings. On these foundations let me erect strong and sturdy pillars of human will to guide me through life undaunted and unafraid. On top of these pillars let me build a roof of discipline. Let me cover this structure with a framework of kindness and joy—and let these walls be expandable so as to reach out and shelter those in need.

Lord, help me to keep building! Never let me be content to sit back and let my house deteriorate. Let me expand always upward—and help me keep my head high so that I may see above the haze of confusion and indecision. But above all, let my front door always remain open and allow fellowship to enter in and cleanse my house of smugness and stagnation.[1]

I think I see,
But sometimes I'm not sure.
I know what I want to see.
I see what I want to see
Sometimes, and it's heavenly.

There are times when my seeing
Seems to be blurry.
And what I look at doesn't interest me;
My real vision is vague.

Does anyone really see
Reality?

1
Mirages in Marriage

IN THE HEAT OF THE DESERT SUN the illusion known as a mirage is common. The tired and thirsty traveler, gazing expectantly toward the horizon, sees what appears to be a pool of life-sustaining water in the distance. Eagerly he presses toward the welcome sight, only to have it vanish from his view. What he has seen was only a trick that his eyes and his mind have played on him.

Marriage has its mirages also. In the heat of infatuation a person may see highly desirable but actually nonexistent qualities in a potential mate, only to have the vision vanish after the wedding. Small wonder that in the United States approximately 500,000 couples end up in the divorce court each year.

Most people look forward to marriage with high hopes, and rightly, for it is an essential part of God's plan for mankind. Not only does it provide for the continuation of the human race and the nurture of children, but it offers the most intimate and rewarding kind of human fellowship as a man and a woman share their love. Why, then, does the vision so often become nothing more than a mirage?

Part of the answer is found in the way we do things in the western world. Unlike the Orient, where marriages are arranged by the families concerned, western couples enjoy the more romantic adventure of seeking and finding each other. In our so-called open society young people are free to pick and choose their mates. They become acquainted at the drug store, at church, at school, at a party, or even perhaps at the bus stop. There are no "off limits" except those built up within the persons themselves, and even these may depend on how lonely the persons feel.

Suppose the all-important meeting happens at a summer resort. It begins by chance, it is confirmed by choice, and it is encouraged by mutual response. There occurs a round of dates—dinners, snacks, amusements, boat rides, walks, and swims together, as through these shared experiences two people deepen their acquaintance with one another—at least insofar as they are ready to be open and honest in their sharing.

Their dating is likely to take on a dreamlike quality, especially if their own self-identity is not clear. In this idealized romantic state a girl may easily fall in love with a boy for the simple reason that he reminds her of a movie hero she idealizes, and consequently she attributes to her beloved some qualities of strength, grace, and humor which really are not there. And he, in turn, overjoyed at the attention he is receiving, reasons that any girl who loves him so much must possess great intelligence and wisdom. In this kind of illusory experience it is not uncommon for a girl blinded in love to choose a mate (over the protests of her friends) who may drink too much and cannot hold down a steady job. And it has been wisely said that many a man who has fallen in love with a dimple has made a mistake by marrying the whole girl.

As one author has put it, many couples feel as though a magic wand has been waved over them and a magic carpet is carrying them toward a delightful new world—but the fact is that soon after the marriage ceremony the magic carpet will be changed to a living room carpet and the wand to a broom.[1] Another has called romantic love "a very unstable, kaleidoscopic experience, fascinating, shifting, immature."[2]

The blindness of those in love may seem amusing to the onlooker, but it is actually no laughing matter. Every prospective marriage partner needs to be alert to it. Psychologists and sociologists say that this highly romanticized idea of love probably causes more heartaches than happiness. The danger is that it does not adequately prepare a couple for the realities of marriage and the consequent responsibilities they will face as the months and years of married life go by.

Another of the mirages that often appear in marriage is the illusion that true love is based entirely upon physical attraction and emotion. When two people experience a happiness together which approaches ecstasy, whether it is rational or not, they feel quite certain that their love is genuine and alive. On the other hand, if disenchantment begins to set in and happiness lags, then they are equally sure that love has died. When this loss occurs during the courtship period, one or both of the persons may feel abandoned and deeply distressed, but the problem is much more serious when it occurs in marriage. Convinced that their marriage is emotionally empty, the couple may decide to part. And, furthermore, it is not uncommon for a second or even a third home to be wrecked along with their own as they seek fulfillment of their frustrated emotions by falling in love with other married persons.

Physical attraction and emotion, important as they are, do not provide in themselves a sufficient basis for a happy marriage. They lead to a fallacious concept of "limited liability." According to this fiction, marriage is an experiment to see whether two people are emotionally suited to one another. The man looks out into the desert and sees his Cinderella in the moonlight, lovely and fair. He walks hand in hand with her into matrimony pledging that she will remain his darling wife "as long as your cooking pleases me, you keep your girlish figure, and you do not make too many demands on my time." This Hollywood philosophy permits changing marriage partners as casually as one would change a suit of clothes. If the match does not measure up to the romantic expectations of one or both persons, it is called off and a trip is made to the divorce court.

Marriage must be more than this. It must grow out of a philosophy of life, seasoned with practical good sense. A happy marriage depends in large measure on one's capacity during courtship to differentiate between true love and mere infatuation.

Love can be compared to flour. Flour is an important ingredient, but by itself it will not make a cake. In addition one needs baking powder, salt, sugar, shortening, eggs, and milk. Love is the chief ingredient for a happy marriage, but it is not the only one. Walter Lippman once said that "love and nothing else soon becomes nothing else." Having a deep religious faith, understanding one's self, and knowing the factors that make for success in marriage are vital. These matters will be considered in the forthcoming chapters.

I know.
Love, when I am with you
The world seems new.
I am awakened to fresh possibility
In all that I see.

I know love.
When I am with you
Riotous beauty comes into view.
It is as if suddenly I am soaring,
Flying free—but with integrity.

I know love when I am with you.
Your presence gives me a clue
To the meaning of life.
When you place your hand in mine
We are one—with the Divine.

I know.

2
The Look of Love

TRYING TO DEFINE LOVE IN A FEW WORDS is almost as difficult as sitting beside a mighty ocean and trying to describe all the nuances of moods which sea and sky inspire. Love, like friendship, must be experienced if one is to know its depth and reality. But this difficulty does not excuse us from trying to describe it, even though we know we will fall short of its full range and scope.

Love is a force that is experienced between man and his fellowman and between man and God. It is a feeling, a sentiment, but it is much more. Our human existence is characterized by the fact that we are alone and alienated from mankind. We cannot bear this separation, and so we are driven by an inner urge to seek relatedness and identification with others. This force manifests itself within mankind in many ways. One of these ways is as a combination of loneliness and sexual desire.

True love heals and creates as it acts through personal relationships. Our loneliness is overcome as we find a worthy object of our love. When we love another person in a mature way, we *respect* him for what he is and as he is. We are concerned about him and will respond to his needs, even beyond our own. At love's fullest and finest we will want to sacrifice even life for him, thus approaching the meaning of the biblical verse, "Greater love has no man than this, that a man lay down his life for his friends" (John 15:13).

Love between a man and a woman is a growing relationship which unfolds increasingly the more they know and understand each other. Before marriage they need to spend as much time as possible together, mutually discussing common problems and ideals, doing things and going places together, and becoming as thoroughly acquainted with each other as possible. One of the wisest sages of our time has said that love as an emotion is not self-sustaining but that it endures only when lovers love many things together, and not merely each other.

A beautiful and prophetic book is the Pulitzer prize-winning novel *To Kill a Mockingbird*, by Harper Lee. This is a story of attorney Atticus Finch, a widower in a southern town, telling of his struggles to raise two children and of his courage in defending a Negro falsely accused of raping a white woman. In one tender scene between "Scout" (Jean Louise, age 8) and her father, the little girl tells Atticus that she does not want to go to school anymore because of the violence and rudeness of one of the boys:

". . . Please don't send me back sir."

Atticus stood up and walked to the end of the porch. When he completed his first examination of the wisteria vine he strolled back to me.

"First of all," he said, "if you can learn a simple trick, Scout, you'll get along a lot better with all kinds of folks. You never really understand a person until you consider things from his point of view—"

"Sir?"

"—until you climb into his skin and walk around in it."[1]

Loving a person is doing just this: considering life from his point of view and putting yourself in his shoes to know how he feels. Empathy, the ability to understand and feel the joys and pains of the other, is the basic art of love.

Because the human personality is so complex, it takes time really to know and understand another person; in fact, this kind of growth is a lifelong proposition. Mature love is not automatic. You do not fall in love—you grow and climb into it. To be responsible in love means to have respect, care, and understanding for the other and to want to do all you can for him. Moreover, not only do we ourselves need to grow in love but we also must help our loved one to grow and to develop his capacities, and we must promote his happiness. Psychiatrist Erich Fromm says, "To love a person productively implies to care and to feel responsible for his life, not only for his physical existence but for the growth and development of all of his human powers."[2]

The emotion of love is not always self-sustaining, but fortunately it can be fed and nurtured and constantly renewed. One way in which a very mature teacher and his wife kept their obligations of love renewed was to read together aloud, at least once a week before going to sleep, the apostle Paul's "Hymn of Love" found in 1 Corinthians 13. This is a good practice which all of us might follow:

Love is patient and kind; love is not jealous or boastful; it is not arrogant or rude. Love does not insist on its own way; it is not irritable or resentful; it does not rejoice at wrong, but rejoices in the right. Love bears all things, believes all things, hopes all things, endures all things. Love never ends. . . .[3]

The late Mrs. Dwight Morrow, just after celebrating her twentieth wedding anniversary, sat next to the great pianist Paderewski at a banquet. She told him of recalling the first time she had heard him perform, when she was just a student sitting high in the gallery at Northampton Academy of Music. He asked whether she had ever returned to her old Alma Mater, and she replied: "Yes, occasionally I like to go back and sit in my old chapel seat and think of how much happier I am now than I ever thought I could have been twenty years ago." The great pianist thoughtfully asked, "You mean you are happier now than you dreamed of being when you were eighteen?" "Yes, I am," she affirmed. Whereupon Paderewski is said to have risen to his feet, bowed slightly in tribute, and exclaimed, "Madame, I would like to meet your husband."[4]

The world is filled with couples who like the Morrows have experienced a growing love, but unfortunately these do not make the headlines as do the marital failures of a glamorous movie star.

Though all of us need to strive toward a mature concept of love, we also need to be realistic enough to recognize that none of us is fully mature. The lofty idealism of love must be counterbalanced by a Christian understanding of human nature. There is a sinful will-to-power in each of us which means that we often assert ourselves at the expense of our loved one. Even at the outset of our love, tensions are present, and they grow all too easily. Who among us, when tired and cranky, has not commiserated with the great apostle who confessed, "For I do not do the good I want, but the evil I do not want is what I do" (Romans 7:19).

To love is risky, because love involves self-giving, which in turn means exposing our true selves to our beloved. Love can be exploited and manipulated, or even unconsciously rejected, with painful and disastrous effects on the self-images and relationships of those concerned. Misused, love can make some people too possessive and others too dependent.

Any two people who have experienced tender feelings of affection toward each other and have committed themselves to marriage need to plant their love squarely in the garden of faith. Both partners to any proposed marriage need to turn to Christ and the church for strength and renewal. They must appropriate the insights of faith and in so doing will place their lives within a "cosmic frame of reference."

In order to transcend the selfish, the lover must be able to have a personal sense of security and a feeling of worth and adequacy, an assurance that he belongs in the universe. If the couple worship regularly together at the church of their choice, this practice will help to fill their lives with power and purpose. It will heal and offer forgiveness for the imperfect expressions of their love. Most of all, it will link their lives to the purposes of God in the world and will give them goals beyond themselves for which to strive. "God is love. . . . We love because he first loved us. . . . This is my commandment, that you love one another as I have loved you" (1 John 4:8, 19; John 16:12).

Home is a haven, a beacon bright
that shines in the night.
Home is a heartbeat that calls the son
to come back on the run.
Home is where prodigals go back.

Home is a horizon, a star afar,
a goal for the soul.
Home is a habit, where beaten and burned
we yearn to return.
Home is where we can be human.

Home is a hymn, a memory-melody
that makes sweet by its beat.
Home is a harmony, where chords are resolved,
and I'm free to be me.
Home is where hurts are healed.

Home is our heaven, a freeing friend,
where we have worth by our birth.
Home is not harsh—it is love-like!
it holds and enfolds.
Home is where God is made real.

3
Our Religious Roots

IN MARRIAGE WE BECOME CO-CREATORS WITH THE DIVINE. Three passages from the opening pages of the Bible help us to become aware of this awesome role. The first is Genesis 1:28, in which God after creating man tells him: "Be fruitful and multiply, and fill the earth and subdue it; and have dominion over the fish of the sea and over the birds of the air and over every living thing that moves on the earth." The second is Genesis 1:31, where we find the great affirmation: "And God saw everything that he had made, and behold, it was very good." And the third is Genesis 2:18, 24, where we read: "Then the Lord God said, 'It is not good that the man should be alone; I will make him a helper fit for him.' . . . Therefore a man

21

leaves his father and his mother and cleaves to his wife, and they become one flesh."

These momentous words establish God's plan for the continued creation and growth of the human race, but the story does not end in this idyllic fashion. When God created this being called man, he did so in his own image; therefore man, like God, must be free—even free to try to be a god himself, though obviously he cannot succeed in such an effort. The man's name is Adam, but this word is really a Hebrew term which we might interpret "every man," and thus we are told that this gift of love and freedom is made to all of us.

Like Adam and Eve in their encounter with the serpent, however, we cannot accept our freedom without misusing it and putting ourselves first, thus corrupting our love. The ancient story of the Fall of Man in the Garden of Eden thus realistically points up the built-in conflict that every human being has to live with—his inability to love adequately and live responsibly. Albert Camus in *The Plague* said, "I know positively . . . that each of us has the plague within him; no one . . . on earth is free from it."[1] Call it "the plague" or whatever you want; there *is* a downward drag in each of us which the theologians call "sin." We are not naturally altruistic; our first love is always ourselves. In spite of the cleverness of human ingenuity, we cannot change this love of self; thus we all participate with Adam and Eve in the Fall.

Because marriage involves fallible people, it too is subject to the Fall—perhaps even more than other human institutions, because of the close proximity of its partners and the intimate nature of the relationship. We therefore need to come to terms with the religious evaluation of sin and its application to marriage. Too many young people caught in the false ideas of the marriage mirage feel that they are different and that the foregoing analysis will not apply to them. Sooner or later, however, they must face the fact that they are not different after all; the problem is universal.

To be religiously mature is to know that we are not sufficient in our own power and wisdom. To be Christianly grown-up means to be able to say humbly with the prodigal son, "Father, I have sinned against heaven and before you: I am no longer worthy to be called

your son" (Luke 15:21). It is this attitude of humility and recep-
tivity which opens the doors to our insight and God's grace.

The good news of the Christian faith is the proclamation that the
God who has created the world has also made adequate provision for
its restoration through Jesus the Christ, his Son. God loved the world
so much that he sent his Son not only to show us the way to freedom
and wholeness but actually to participate in the fallen order and to
enter our lives through his abiding Spirit. The apostle Paul described this relationship as "Christ . . . formed in you" (Galatians
4:19). Thus God's Holy Spirit (the spirit of Jesus released from
time and space) comes into a believer's life. God sees not the man's
bungling and sinful life but rather Christ in its place. He sees man
not as he is but as he will become: perfect as Christ is perfect.

Because of Christ's spirit in the life of a believer, God accepts and
forgives us in spite of our unacceptability; his love claims us in spite
of our unloveliness. Being accepted and forgiven and loved, we have
an important status and security which the world cannot give, and
consequently we are able to overcome our anxieties and be free from
meaninglessness.

The grace of God in giving himself for us is a gift beyond human
repayment. When we are able to accept God's acceptance, we are
actually accepting life as it is and ourselves as we really are. No longer
do we have to mask our pretended goodness. We can courageously
accept ourselves and can then therefore authentically accept another
person the way he is.

There is one more aspect to the Christian good news which has
practical application to married life. To accept in faith the proclamation that God has raised Christ from the dead means that the God
to whom we give our allegiance is the all-powerful Lord of history
who cannot be defeated or have his will thwarted by the worst that
the forces of evil can accomplish here in this world. As we surrender
our whole selves and put our lives in loving trust in his care, we
experience a new sense of security in the confidence of God's mighty
power! In gratitude for the freeing love God has graciously bestowed
upon us, we are able to rejoice in all that life brings. This awareness
that God is in control enables us to respond creatively to sickness and

trouble, for we know that nothing in the world can separate us from God's love, not even death. As the apostle Paul has expressed it in Romans 14:7-9:

> None of us lives to himself, and none of us dies to himself. If we live, we live to the Lord, and if we die, we die to the Lord; so then, whether we live or whether we die, we are the Lord's. For to this end Christ died and lived again, that he might be Lord both of the dead and of the living.

The biblical faith will not come to everyone in the same manner, but God himself is always in some way present, quickening and empowering the believer to a new freedom and a more responsible love. An intelligent understanding and participation in the life, death, and living spirit of Christ helps us to attain a new level of maturity toward our marriage mate, our family, and our ever-widening circle of neighbors. An awareness of the deep meaning of the cross keeps us from feeling superior or "lording it over" our marriage partner. The presence of Christ's spirit in our lives gives us a meaningful new frame of reference and security, so that we no longer have to go around trying to manipulate or "use" other people to compensate for our own insecurity. Knowing that our husband or wife is one for whom Christ also died means that we have a loving responsibility toward him (or her). We can accept this person and put up with his irksome qualities because we know acceptance is exactly how God *has acted* and *is acting* toward us.

"Beloved, let us love one another," we read in 1 John 4:7. To grow in love is the hope and purpose of a newly-married couple or one about to be married. Love is learned. It is learned from mature, loving persons who care about us. Those who are fortunate enough to have had such parents have been influenced since childhood to be outgoing, loving persons. Others have learned the spiritual meaning of love from persons outside the family who have cared about them. In the same way a husband and a wife, as they mutually express their concern and affection, can help each other to grow in love.

There are religious roots which will help us to grow in love, and it is imperative that we appropriate these for ourselves. None of us is fully mature. Psychology has helped us to understand that in loving we often express hostility and jealousy toward those we really care about. This attitude is called "ambivalence." As a result we feel guilty, but our Christian faith provides the means to rid ourselves of this guilt. In marriage our faith should become a joint concern. Through prayer and worship we are made aware of the forgiving grace of God that comes to us as in the experience of the father and the prodigal son: "But while he was yet at a distance, his father saw him and had compassion, and ran and embraced him and kissed him" (Luke 15:20).

A Christian in marriage is one who knows the depth of his sin and estrangement, but he also knows the nature of the forgiveness of God and has tasted the sweet joy of forgiveness himself. In any consideration of marriage from a Christian standpoint one must cultivate the roots of religion or else we foster what Elton Trueblood has called a "cut-flower civilization." Marriage cut off from its Judeo-Christian roots, like a flower severed from its source of sustenance, cannot long endure.

We live in an age
of status and speed,
of glamor and go.
So how do we find a mate?

Turn on the computer,
set the dial for "ideal,"
wait for the machine
to turn out "a queen"?
No.

A lifetime love
must be like a melody
yet possess fidelity,
and share similar
tastes and tones and tears.

We must make this choice
skillfully and willfully
and with prayer-power;
Then pledge to please throughout the years.

4

Backgrounds Are Basic

MARRIAGES ARE NOT MADE IN HEAVEN, but if we use our God-given intelligence wisely we can make our marriages heavenly. Every contemplated marriage requires adjustments and a careful coming-to-terms with the romantic mirages we noted in chapter one. The time to talk about these things is before the ship of matrimony has gotten under way, not afterward.

A Christian marriage is one where both partners consciously attempt to carry out their union within a Christian orientation. Each must accept the resources of the Christian faith and apply these to the new life which is being undertaken together. Christian marriage is an adventure in creative love lived in freedom and supported by the fellowship of the Christian church. There is no precise doctrinal path to be pursued, no formula to be followed. Rather there is a *basic commitment* to be made, a covenant to be entered into, involving God and you and your loved one, with God at the top of this triangle.

Among other things, a Christian marriage requires three pledges, of which the first has to do with *fidelity*. In the marriage ceremony each is asked to commit himself to be faithful, come what may: "Will you be true . . . in sickness and health, in sorrow and joy?" Once during a premarital counseling interview when the above phrase was read, a young army private loudly remarked, "That sure covers a lot of territory!" He was absolutely right—it does. Unlike the romantic mirage which equates love *only* with feeling, the Christian concept bases love on faithfulness, which *includes* feeling. We are able to love because God first loved us. If God is your partner, you have a powerful ally in helping you to be true. The Christian pledge has been paraphrased by Andre Maurois in words something like these: "I have chosen; from now on my aim will be not to search for someone else who will please me, but to please the one I have chosen."

The second pledge has to do with *finality*. "What God has truly joined together no man can put asunder." When a Christian enters marriage, he enters it for life. He undertakes an *un*limited liability for his marriage mate. When this permanent commitment is made, deep trust and security will pervade the relationship, encouraging a "second mile" effort to overcome the problems and crises which are bound to come when the honeymoon is over.

There is one more pledge in Christian marriage and that is *mutuality*. This is expressed in Ephesians 5:21-33, where the apostle Paul compares marriage to the love Christ has for his bride, the church. The wife is full of faith in her husband "as to the Lord," and the husband is to be faithful as he merits his wife's trust. As Christ gave himself for his bride, the church, so the Christian husband is to love and honor his bride. The key to a Christian approach to mutuality is found in the 21st verse, "Be subject to one another out of reverence for Christ."

When two people commit themselves "as unto the Lord" and enter into matrimony with fidelity, finality, and mutuality, they begin to do more than just associate with each other. As the weeks and months go by, spiritually and emotionally they cease being separate individuals and become one. This is the miracle of marriage. "For this reason a man shall leave his father and mother and be joined to his wife, and the two shall become one" (Matthew 19:5).

You will want to ask each other some searching questions about your feelings concerning these pledges. Do you have any serious reservations about the commitment? If so, these may well be discussed with your pastor. If you have not already scheduled a series of meetings with him, you might use these as a way of beginning the first interview.

Backgrounds are basic, and your marriage will have a much better chance to succeed if you as a couple can thoroughly encounter and explore one another's thinking and attitudes about the problems you soon will be facing.

A helpful procedure is to take a simple test. An excellent set of test questions has been prepared by Dr. Granger E. Westberg, chaplain of the Augustana Hospital in Chicago, Illinois.[1] This excellent little inventory is not designed to answer your questions, but merely to raise some basic issues and alert you to possible points of friction. Dr. Westberg says that the score is not important. The purpose is to "eliminate the lecture form of premarital counseling."

In case your minister does not have a test available, the following are some important questions to raise with one another and discuss with him:

1. Are you both Christians? Do you both have a working knowledge of the Bible? If you are not now members of the same church, do you plan to bring your membership together?
2. Should you have children? How many?
3. How about finances? Will the wife work? Do either of you have any debts? Have you carefully worked out a budget?
4. Where will you live after marriage? With either family?
5. What is your attitude toward sex? How about birth control? Have you read a good book on the subject recently?[2] Is the woman planning to have a thorough physical examination before the wedding? Is the man?
6. Are both of you acquainted with both sets of parents? Do either

of you have any problems with any of the parents? If so, how will you deal with these problems?

7. What type of wedding will you want? Whom are you planning to invite? Will you desire a double-ring ceremony?

Since backgrounds are basic, let us explore some of the knotty areas of tension which researchers have discovered are critical issues in determining whether marriages fail or succeed.

The first and rather obvious problem is whether you are both of the same faith. We began this chapter with a definition of Christian marriage. Obviously if one of you is a non-Christian or a nonbeliever, the conditions set down will be difficult to accept. Marriage is a covenant with God which in its most profound level speaks a language of religious ecstasy and communion. If you have not both become sensitive to this Christian view of life, you may not be able to become "one flesh" in the deepest sense of marriage. A mixed marriage does not automatically fail, of course, but it does involve serious obstacles, and statistics show that the chances of success are poorer than when the two partners share the same faith.

A mixed marriage can present all kinds of difficulties. In some cases the parents of one partner have refused to attend the wedding if it has been held in the other's church, and this, naturally, gets the relationship off to a poor start. There may be difficult social adjustments to friends. A conflict of interest is likely to materialize over the giving of money to church if the other partner is a nonbeliever. If one is a Roman Catholic there is the question of birth control, and this may have far-reaching implications in the couple's sex relations. However, the really major divisive aspect of a Protestant-Catholic partnership is centered in the children. The Roman Church asks the Protestant to sign an agreement that the children will be brought up in the Catholic religion if the other spouse is to remain in good standing with his church.[3]

There is so much conflict and tension in an interfaith marriage that often the couple feel it is not worth the struggle and stop going to any church whatsoever. Some marriage counselors are frank in advising persons from different faiths to break up before they become too emotionally involved. This advice may be more easily given than followed. In some instances it may be sound counsel, but in any case Bishop James Pike of the Protestant Episcopal Church has expressed the feeling of most churchmen in these words:

> *The solution, in a nutshell, is this:* each of the parties, forgetting what he or she was born and forgetting what his parents are, should rethink his or her religious position in terms of what each really believes and what Church most nearly represents that actual belief. . . . If, however, this honest reconsideration leads both to conviction as to a faith that happens to be already that of one of the two parties, both should have the humility to make possible the conversion of the heretofore outsider to this faith without any sense of having "yielded" to the other. In no case should one yield to the other; both should yield to the claims of truth as they have worked it out through honest study, soul searching and decision.[4]

The biblical rationale for the bishop's words is found in Jesus' parable in Luke 14:28: "For which of you, desiring to build a tower, does not first sit down and count the cost, whether he has enough to complete it?" It is far better for a couple to count the cost before than to realize afterwards that they lacked enough common grounds to make a success of their marriage.

In this day of racial revolution the question of interracial marriage is often raised. Let it be stated that this is not a religious problem, for the Bible clearly says that God's love goes out to all races and he shows no partiality (Acts 10:34-35). In some states, however, there are legal barriers. Furthermore, an interracial couple may run into many social obstacles. Housing may be difficult to obtain, and there are always the accentuated "in-law problems" of any intercultural marriage. In most academic communities and many big cities there is an increasing climate of acceptance toward racially mixed couples. In short, every marriage requires adjustments but a racially mixed marriage has the normal variety plus additional tensions brought about by cultural resistance. If such a couple is to find happiness and success in marriage, both persons must be very mature and devoted individuals who have carefully considered all the problems involved in their decision.

Another issue is that of in-laws. Should you live with either family? The answer which most marriage experts give is a categorical "no." If at all possible, avoid such an arrangement in the early days of your wedded life. "A man leaves his father and his mother and cleaves to his wife." These words from Genesis 2:24 make a great deal of sense. As is well known, adjusting to each other in the first months of marriage is apt to be a difficult and delicate process. You need privacy in which to work out the differences of opinion which are bound to come up; the presence of a third party (either parent) may adversely influence the solution and is almost certain to increase the tension. In spite of the fact that you may have to start out modestly, your own living quarters seem advisable.

Even though you make a decision not to live with either family, you will have to make some other decisions about in-laws. Maybe both of you have been blessed by loving and mature parents. If so they will respect your freedom and privacy. Nevertheless, tension often arises after the wedding when the mother of the bride or groom visits the young couple and in an honest attempt to be helpful will actually interfere with the running of the household. Without ever meaning to hurt, she may criticize the bride's cooking or the way she runs her household. By considering these problems ahead of time and discussing your plans with your in-laws, you can in a loving and firm manner issue your marital "declaration of independence."

As Christians we are directed to follow the fifth commandment by honoring our parents. A time may come when, because of old age, sickness, or some unexpected crisis, you will have to take care of one or more of your parents. You should mentally prepare yourselves for this kind of service, and if and when the need comes you should honorably and cheerfully do what is necessary to help. Until such time—especially in the early years of marriage—you will want to follow the paraphrasing of our Lord's teaching: "No woman can serve two masters, that is, she cannot serve mother and husband." Most in-laws, of course, are a tremendous help to newlyweds, rather than a hindrance, but the best relationship is one in which everybody's position is clearly understood.

By this time in your going together you have probably talked over many things and have given much thought to the values, interests, and common goals you share. Needless to say these are very important.

However, many couples enter marriage without really having explored their backgrounds, and this lack can be tragic. If courtship has been nothing more than "dancing and romancing," it may have been quite thrilling but it has not intelligently prepared the couple for the problems of married life.

One more suggestion: Do not try to reform one another. It is better to accept each *as you are*. As Jeremiah observed long ago, a leopard does not change his spots (*Pygmalion* and *My Fair Lady* to the contrary). A few habits may be altered, but only with difficulty. If you think you are going to change each other's basic outlook or orientation toward life, you are probably doomed to failure. The watermark in a piece of writing paper cannot be changed by rubbing the surface, nor a person's cultural conditioning of a lifetime altered by a wife's or husband's nagging. Instead of reforming, you may break up your marriage. Naturally you both can grow and mature together, but this process usually results not from nagging but from a positive feeling of mutual respect and the religious acceptance of higher goals.

Marriages are not made in heaven, but God has endowed us with feelings and brains so that we can intelligently assess the characteristics of those to whom we are attracted. Many times it is the little things which make or break a marriage.

In the Pacific Northwest a great tree fell to the ground. It had endured storms and floods for generations. In the end what made it fall was not the earthquakes and hurricanes and lightning, but little insects. They had bored beneath the bark and cut into the fibers and eaten away the great tree's heart. As a result, the mighty king of the forest fell.

Have you talked about the possible insects that may eat into and destroy your relationship together? Backgrounds are basic!

Red-haired Helen,
Helen, my light,
Where, oh, where
Will you be tonight?

Feel the sharp staccato rhythm!
Hear the weird watusi wail!
Will your blind lover laud you
As he adumbrates his braille?

Helen, my love—
Red is your hair—
Where are you going
Where, oh, where?

Sense the slipstream on your forehead,
Jaguar jets to splendid speed!
Will your blind lover save you
On his supersonic steed?

Red-haired Helen,
Helen, my sorrow,
Where, oh, where
Will you be tomorrow?

5
Maturity Means Discipline

ONE CANNOT SPEAK ABOUT LOVE AND THE FAMILY without dealing
with the question of sex. There has been a dense smog of misinforma-
tion and confusion abroad, and Christians need to have a forthright
and honest presentation of the subject.

Fortunately, there are fresh breezes today which are beginning to
blow away some of the shame and guilt connected with sex, and
praise God for this! In the past, people have been made to feel that
sex is dirty and uncouth, not a fit topic even to discuss. The church
was partly responsible for this unfortunate attitude, because for

years it automatically and wrongly associated sex with sin. Today the pendulum has swung far in the other direction. Led by Freud and Kinsey, people have come to regard sex as natural, good, and fun. The Victorian and Puritan myths have been debunked, and the modern novelist, playwright, and song writer have unfurled new banners stamped by such labels as "realism," "honesty," and "freedom." As with all new movements in revolt, we must beware that the pendulum can swing too far. What on the surface may seem to be an emancipation may be a danger. To consider sex the only worthy goal in life is to depersonalize love.

One of the most stark and brutal examples of this "sex for its own sake" thinking is found in Arthur Miller's play *Death of a Salesman.* The chief character is a pathetic man named Willy Loman, a traveling salesman. There is one scene that is particularly poignant. Willy's son Biff, a high school athletic hero, has gotten into trouble and needs the help of his father. He goes to Boston and, to his horror, catches his dad in an act of adultery in a hotel room with a strange woman. In this tragic moment, as Biff stands outside the hotel room door in utter shock, Willy pathetically tries to explain: "She's nothing to me, Biff. I was lonely, I was terribly lonely."[1]

Today's mass media have falsely spelled love with three letters, SEX. This is part of the mirage discussed in chapter one. If we identify love as sex and nothing more, then by the same premise we have to say that the red rooster with his harem of one hundred hens is a tremendous lover!

If Christians looking toward marriage are to be able to withstand the confusing barrage of erotic music, literature, and art from our sex-saturated society, they will have to be armed with the best insights from sociology and psychology, backed up by a well-informed biblical faith.

Let us turn to the wisdom of the Bible. There we find Jesus quoting from an early account of creation to the effect that marriage has been ordained by God, and when a man and his wife leave their parents they become, in fact, one (Matthew 19:5-6). On another occasion he says that love involves the total response of a person's being—his heart, soul, strength, and mind—emotional, spiritual, physical, and mental (Luke 10:27). From these two passages we are able to understand that sex is a God-given fact of nature. God has ordained sex in marriage for the primary purpose of procreation, the creating of new life. But this is not all. Sex is also a means of communicating. The touch of a loved one communicates more than a million words. God's gift of sex is something to be gratefully accepted and enjoyed.

From the apostle Paul we obtain a different and shocking insight. Quoting from the same Old Testament passage that Jesus did, Paul said that if a man has sex relations with a prostitute, he still becomes "one" with her, no matter how meaningless were his intentions of affection (1 Corinthians 6:16). He is saying that sexual intercourse deeply affects the lives of two people and leaves a lasting mark, be it good or bad. This insight, coming many centuries before the science of depth psychology, has been confirmed again and again by psychiatrists and marriage counselors.

With penetrating realism the writers of the Bible thus cut through the clutter of mirages about romantic love to tell us that sex is one of the deepest and most involved psychological experiences which two persons can enter, and furthermore that it makes a lasting union. In a day when sex is taken so lightly it behooves us to stop and take a long hard look at these facts.

In marriage a man and a woman choose one another to share in a lifetime of living, and in sexual intercourse they can share the deepest joys of that life. Through sex God has provided a wonderful language of love by which they can come to know one another and accept each other without guilt.

Now we come to a question that almost every couple awaiting marriage has asked: "Why not sexual intercourse before the wedding? We know we are in love and we have committed ourselves to one another." Here again it is necessary to speak out forthrightly. Although ethically there is a country mile between being promiscuous and being engaged, there are still some serious arguments in favor of premarital chastity.

The pull of sex in a couple can be likened to a mighty river. It must be controlled and channeled, or else like a river at flood time it can overflow its banks and do much damage. How you will act in any given situation is determined largely by the decisions you have made and the attitudes you have formed before the situation arises.

The most important argument in favor of chastity is not that premarital sex usually cannot be carried on in the privacy it needs, nor that there is an inhibiting fear of pregnancy, nor that there is risk of detection. The real danger is that *your marriage may not take place!*

The price which many engaged lovers are forced to pay for giving in to the powerful urges of sex is a loss of zest for the enjoyment of other activities. In some instances, it results in feelings of crudeness. In others—especially on the part of a woman—there may be a feeling of "second-handedness." Here are the findings of a nationally known expert in the field of marriage:

> For every possible gain . . . [of having premarital sex relations] there is a possible loss. The boy may or may not love and respect his sweetheart for having gone all the way before marriage. He may find that his feelings for his sweetheart are no longer so intense now that he has had her sexually. He may feel dissatisfaction arising from the clandestine nature of their coming together. . . . It is possible that he feels guilty about taking advantage of his sweetheart's love, especially if she had been a virgin.

A specific instance is cited:

> One couple have gone steady for a long while. They feel genuine love for one another. For some months now they have been sleeping together several times a week. Now they both report that the glow has gone, and they are at the point of breaking up. She feels cheated that all he wants to do is "eat and fall into bed together" . . . He finds her less attractive now that he knows her intimately.[2]

Sexual experience before the wedding—even if the relationship does not break up—is not good preparation for marriage. Other marriage experts warn that sexual intimacy can prevent a couple from grappling realistically with their problems. Many times quarrels are ended not by facing issues and dealing with them squarely but by smothering one another with kisses. The real danger is that premarital sex relations can become a way of avoiding these issues altogether.

Never let it be said that it is easy for a couple to postpone fulfillment of the deep desire for physical expression of their spiritual unity. Every lover has experienced this conflict. What makes it even more difficult is what Peter Bertocci has called the "sexual progression." This means that the physical expression of sex which is satisfying to a couple at one stage becomes inadequate and needs further stimulation to maintain the same thrill. Holding hands moves on to kissing and caressing. "Thus, the individual is tempted to move from one rung of the ladder of satisfaction to another. . . . He will gradually be led (if he is not willing to forgo further satisfaction) to the point where no action short of sexual intercourse itself is physically and psychologically satisfying."[3] This progression is not inevitable, but all who are deeply in love must recognize it and cope with it.

Here are some practical suggestions which can be followed to avoid getting into situations where undue sexual stimulation is felt by both:

1. Accentuate the positive when you are together by engaging in the kinds of activities where you will not have long hours of isolated and built-in temptations for love making.

2. Participate in sports, hobbies, music, and group fun.

3. Make a wide circle of friends, rather than limiting your associations to just one other couple.

4. Practice sublimating your sexual desires by substituting discussions, walks, and other creative activities. In other words, devise ways of saying "I love you" other than close physical intimacy. Lovers who learn to talk to one another about a variety of subjects are creating a firm foundation for communication in marriage. As Thomas Jefferson wisely said, "If the channels of communication are kept open, truth and righteousness will ultimately prevail."

Christian maturity in love means helping the other person to grow, and not asking: "What can I get from him?" Human beings reach biological maturity in early adolescence, but they attain emotional and spiritual maturity only when they are able to accept responsibility for the welfare of another person. If you as a couple in love can delay your sexual intercourse until after the wedding, you can concentrate on the personal and social needs of one another. This inner discipline and control can strengthen the respect and love between the two of you and will lead to a fuller expression of both personalities in marriage.

Much of what has been said here has been pointed toward chastity as a goal before marriage. What about those who have already gone "all the way?" If the case for self-discipline has been convincing, does this drive the unchaste into despair? Not at all. The last word of the Christian gospel is never one of judgment or condemnation. Whether we are chaste or not, we are all sinners and we need the word which God offers us—the word of *forgiveness*. In the episode of Jesus and the woman taken in adultery (John 8:3-11), he did not cast her away in anger; rather he accepted her with the forgiving words: "Neither do I condemn you; go, and do not sin again."

In this spirit God offers forgiveness to those who are genuinely sorry for their actions. Forgiveness is not easy, as we are painfully reminded by the cross. To receive God's pardon we do not have to become pure (who can?); we only have to admit our need. This is the glory of the good news.[4] When God with his word of forgiveness accepts us in spite of our moral unacceptability, and we receive this gift in humility and openness, we become truly new creatures. We become free—free from the guilt of our sin and free to be responsible toward our loved one. Again we turn to Jesus' great words, "Greater love has no man than this, that a man lay down his life for his friends" (John 15:13). Being forgiven means that once more we are free to love without guilt. But in this light how does a person lay down his life? Not by going out and committing suicide, but by asking his beloved, "How can I serve you? How can we help each other to find strength in the years ahead?"

A fanfare fills the church with brassy blasts;
The congregation stands to greet the groom,
Then turns to toast the entourage. It lasts
Until the bride in rapturous radiance looms
And makes a joyous journey down the aisle.
The faltering father finds his voice at last;
He bravely cuts the cord with tearful smile
And puts her hand in his; the die is cast.
They stand with stern resolve to voice the vows;
With high expectancy their spirits soar:
A mutual trust is what the Lord allows,
And love that's pledged to last forevermore.
> *Dear God, these two frail lovers make this plea,*
> *That what they pledged will last eternally.*

6
Wedding Bells

MARRIAGE CAN BE LIKENED TO AN ADVENTUROUS JOURNEY which you and your beloved are taking together. Like all expeditions it requires much preparation. You are now coming up to the time for the wedding, and you will need to do some very thoughtful planning.

You will find that your pastor will be of inestimable value to you, and as you meet with him from time to time you should not hesitate to ask him anything that comes to your mind about wedding procedures. After all, he has been especially trained in this area. He may ask you to help him by filling out a form giving pertinent information for the wedding (such as the one in the appendix of this book).

PLANNING FOR THE WEDDING

Traditionally speaking, the bride has always taken the lead in preparing for the wedding. Nowadays, however, with the increased emphasis on the sharing of responsibilities in all aspects of marriage, the groom will also want to take part in the planning, at least in the initial stages. Right at the outset let it be said that, as the bride and groom, this is *your* wedding. Your desires and feelings, not those of

other people, are the ones which are important. If you have not carefully thought out your philosophy of marriage and what this implies
with regard to the various arrangements for the wedding, it is likely
that your friends, your parents, and your relatives (with all good
intentions) will make the decisions for you. And there is at least a
fifty-fifty chance that they will pressure you into doing things that
later you may regret.

Most weddings since World War II have been double-ring ceremonies. You will want to decide whether this is your choice also. If
each of you wears a ring, it will be a constant reminder of the pledge
of love you have made to each other in the presence of God. Like
many wedding customs, the ring has a pagan background. It harks
back to the time when the woman was regarded as a chattel (prop-
erty) of the man, and the ring was a sign of her dependence. Christianity, however, has taken the ring and infused it with a new and
sacred meaning. It is now a symbol of the union into which the
couple has entered, an outward and visible token of an inward and
invisible pledge. The round shape implies the eternal origin and
endlessness of their love, and the gold symbolizes the purity which
God brings to a happy marriage.

Most important, a double-ring ceremony symbolizes the mutuality
which we considered in chapter four. In the Christian framework of
marriage there is no double standard of either privilege or responsibility. The two persons are one, united in love:

> There is neither Jew nor Greek, there is neither slave nor free, there is
> neither male nor female; for you are all one in Christ Jesus (Galatians 3:28).

If you are planning a large formal wedding, you will need to clear
dates far in advance. It will be important to reserve the church
sanctuary and the hall in which the reception is to take place. If
special meals are to be served, the caterer's time will have to be
booked early. The pastor is certainly entitled to the courtesy of entering the date in his appointment book well ahead of time.

As soon as practicable, you will want to arrange a "summit conference" with both sets of parents to work out the many mutual prob-

lems in regard to the forthcoming event. If all of you live in or near the same community, this will probably present no particular problem. If not, every effort should still be made to get the two families together for a conversation when possible.

Your wedding is one of the main events not only in your own life but in the lives of others in your family. In fact, if you happen to be the youngest daughter or the only child, it marks a pivotal point in your parents' married lives. They will measure that event as a milestone in their journey through life. Knowing that you will be transferring your basic dependence away from them may hit them rather hard emotionally. They are likely to have mixed feelings, and these will come to the surface every now and then. In a sense they are losing a child, but hopefully they will be dominated by the more mature view that they are gaining a son or daughter.

As you realize, any wedding is not only a religious experience but also a social event of considerable interest to the whole community. Your parents will be well aware of this fact—possibly too much so. It is quite pathetic when in some weddings the social ambitions of the bride's or groom's parents dictate everything, and the wishes of the couple themselves are crushed underfoot. This eventuality should not under any circumstances be allowed to happen, and it will not if you take a firm but loving stand.

Traditionally, the bride's parents pay the major share of the expenses of the wedding, and this responsibility can be quite costly. You may want to keep the expenses down, depending upon the financial circumstances of your family, and such a decision is understandable and wise. A great deal of money can be spent unnecessarily on extras such as musicians, caterers, flowers, and so on. True friends are not offended by simplicity, and as one writer has put it, "People are more important than punch."

Expenses of the wedding should be divided between the bride's family and the groom. The family of the bride should arrange and pay the cost of (1) the invitations and announcements, (2) the bride's trousseau and wedding gown, (3) the bride's luncheon and personal gifts to her maid of honor and bridesmaids, (4) all decorations, (5) the reception, (6) the music, the sexton, and all expenses at the church, except the gift to the minister, (7) the groom's ring, and (8) the photographer. The groom should make arrangements and pay for (1) the rehearsal dinner and special gifts to the ushers and best man, (2) the license, (3) his wedding present to the bride, (4) the wedding ring, (5) the bride's bouquet, the bouquets for the maid of honor and bridesmaids, the boutonnieres for the best man and ushers, and the corsages for his own mother and mother of the bride, (6) a gift to the pastor, and (7) expenses of the honeymoon.

Aside from the matter of cost, there is the question of serving alcoholic beverages, especially champagne. There are some relatives and friends who will doubtless expect liquor and will be disappointed if it is not served. On the other hand, there may be total abstainers present who will be offended by the serving of alcohol. Furthermore, most churches will disapprove of the use of alcoholic refreshments in their social halls. The Christian faith has never dealt in absolutes on this question and there is no biblical prohibition except for drunkenness. Therefore various Christians in good conscience hold a variety of opinions on the subject. However, the apostle Paul put forth sound counsel when he said that if drinking of alcohol is offensive to some or will cause a weak brother to stumble, then it ought to be discreetly omitted (Romans 14:21).

Not everyone will agree on the arrangements for the wedding, and some minor disagreements are normal and inevitable because of differences in ages and customs of the two generations represented. The couple's area of responsibility is primarily with the wedding ceremony and the bridal party; the parents are probably more concerned about which relatives and friends are to be included in the invitation list, and about various details of the reception, the meals, and the housing of friends, relatives, and guests. If friction should appear, a little give-and-take on the part of all is important to keep down any misunderstanding and resentment. A good rule in wedding planning is to keep the lines of communication open. Make sure everyone knows what the plans are.

If you are sending out formal invitations, both families will want to contribute names. Here is another task which will need plenty of time in advance of the wedding. Tradition has dictated that there should be one list of persons to be invited to the reception, another containing those who will attend the ceremony only, and a third of persons who will receive only a wedding announcement rather than an invitation. In recent years, however, this tradition has been yielding to the more informal practice of sending no invitations but rather placing advance announcements in the local newspapers and in the church calendar, indicating that the church is open to all of the couple's friends who would like to attend the wedding. This does away with the distasteful distinctions and the flip-a-coin choices as to who should and should not be invited. It opens the doors in welcome to anyone who is sufficiently interested in your wedding to want to come.

There is a correlation between invitations sent and gifts received, and maybe you will have some strong feelings on this subject pro or con. It is true that a person who receives an invitation does feel an obligation to send a gift, and some unscrupulous couples have exploited this. However, it is comforting to know that many do not send gifts unless they wish to do so, and to them an invitation or the lack of one does not affect their desire to give. Most of the gifts you will receive are tangible expressions of affection to you and your family.

It is a good idea to keep a record of your wedding presents as they arrive. Most bookstores sell record books for this purpose, or you can improvise your own from a notebook. Such books are conveniently lined for entering the nature of the present, the date received, the name and address of the sender, and the name of the shop from which it came. Keeping this record makes possible the exchange of duplicate presents and provides a helpful memorandum for the years ahead. Even more important, it is an aid to the bride as she carries out her pleasant but essential task of writing personal notes of thanks for all of the gifts. It is much wiser to keep up with the thank-you notes as the gifts arrive and not allow unacknowledged presents to accumulate. Customarily a room in the bride's home is set aside for showing the gifts to guests who come to the house. However, the bride's trousseau (consisting of personal linen, clothing, and blankets) is not displayed.

You probably will want photographs to commemorate your wedding. If you are going to employ a professional photographer, this is another one of the many details you will want to arrange for ahead of time. In lieu of a professional, however, you can have friends or relatives take pictures for you. This is one of the ways you can cut expenses. Regardless of who will be taking the pictures, you will not want the ceremony itself marred by popping flash bulbs, so make sure this prohibition is quite clear. Perhaps you can have the pastor include this request in his opening remarks to the bridal party at the rehearsal. He can then include the instructions that after the ceremony is concluded and the congregation has dispersed, you will all return to the chancel of the church to pose for pictures.

In most churches there are set rules about the use of the pipe organ. This is one of the many matters you will want to talk over with the pastor.

The deep significance of the wedding ceremony and the dignity of the church sanctuary should be the basic guides to the selection of suitable music for the occasion. The purpose is to establish a mood of worship while the guests are being seated and to prepare them for the sacred rite. Thus the music should never be trivial nor should it be in the so-called "popular" vein. Since the occasion is a joyous one, this feeling can be reflected in the choice of music. The selections listed below by organist George Oplinger[1] have been found to fulfill these purposes. From the list, which is by no means complete, an worshipful and appropriate half-hour program prior to the ceremony can be chosen.

T. Arne: "Flute Solo"
J. S. Bach: "In Thee Is Gladness," "Jesu, Joy of Man's Desiring," "Now Thank We All Our God," "Rejoice Ye Christians," "Sheep May Safely Graze," "Sinfonia, Wedding Cantata No. 196"
C. Balbastre: "Prelude in Two Noels"
J. Bonnet: "Pastorale," "Romance sans Paroles"
J. Brahms: "A Lovely Rose Is Blooming"
D. Buxtehude: "How Brightly Shines the Morning Star"
G. Edmundson: "Fairest Lord Jesus"
C. Franck: "Fantasia in C" (1st movement)
A. Guilmant: "Pastorale" (1st Sonata)

G. F. Handel: "The Faithful Shepherd"
J. Jongen: "Chant de Mai"
P. Martini: "Gavotte"
J. J. McGrath: "Arioso"
M. Reger: "Benedictus," "Melodia"
P. Warlock: "Andante Tranquillo"
Ch. M. Widor: "Andante Cantabile, 4th Symphony"
R. Vaughan Williams: "Rhosymedre"
S. Wright: "Brother James' Air"

Vocal music is often desired and, if the selections are appropriate, can contribute much to the atmosphere of worship. The same rules apply here as for the choice of the preludial organ music. The vocal selections usually are scheduled just before and/or after the bride's mother is seated. If desired, a suitable vocal number may be used during the ceremony. Some suggestions are:

J. S. Bach: "My Heart Ever Faithful," "Jesu Joy of Man's Desiring"
J. Barnby: "Sandringham" (hymn tune)
J. Clokey: "O Perfect Love"
C. Franck: "O Lord Most Holy"
E. Grieg: "I Love Thee"
H. S. Oakeley: "Abends" (hymn tune)
R. Vaughan Williams: "Down Ampney" (hymn tune)
H. Willan: "Eternal Love"

The wedding processional and recessional should maintain the reverence and dignity befitting the sacred rite of marriage. Like any other church procession, it should not be "marched." The bridal party should enter and leave the sanctuary naturally, walking unhurriedly and in a dignified manner. Although the familiar "Lohengrin" and "Midsummer Night's Dream" marches have been used, their operatic nature lacks the desired dignity and their use is being discouraged. Some of the more appropriate selections follow:

Processional

L. Boellmann: "Prelude, Suite Gothique"
J. Clokey: "Processional"
G. F. Handel: "March, Occasional Oratorio"
J. J. McGrath: "Processional"
H. Purcell: "Largo, 12th Sonata," "Trumpet Voluntary"

Recessional

A. Campra: "Rigaudon"
G. F. Handel: "Grand Chorus, from 'Joshua,' " "The Rejoicing"
S. Karg-Elert: "Now Thank We All Our God"
J. J. McGrath: "Recessional"
H. Purcell: "Trumpet Voluntary," "Trumpet Tune"

A formal wedding is customarily preceded by the bride's luncheon for her bridesmaids and the groom's dinner for his ushers, or a combination dinner for both. The wedding party may consist of from two to ten bridesmaids and an equal number of ushers. These are usually invited from among the friends and classmates of the couple.

THE REHEARSAL

The rehearsal will probably be conducted the night before the wedding, but the time is optional, depending upon when all or most of the wedding party can be present. This will be an occasion of genuine joy mixed with seriousness. You will not want to be long-faced about it, but neither will you want the members of your wedding party to be so frivolous that they get out of hand and forget that they are rehearsing a religious service.

As soon as all the participants have arrived, the pastor (who is in charge) may set the tone of the rehearsal by having everyone come to the front of the church while he explains thoroughly and reverently the proceedings of the ceremony. This statement will clarify the mechanics of the wedding, but, more important, it will go a long way toward eliminating the possible horseplay which tends to take place as people try to cover up nervous tension.

The pastor may begin the rehearsal by having the bridal party stand before the altar or communion table in the position where they will find themselves after the processional march. He then reads the ceremony in its entirety, explaining the details as he goes along, such as the passing of the bouquets from bride to maid of honor to bridesmaid, the lifting of the bride's veil, and the passing of the rings from best man and maid of honor to the groom and bride respectively. He then has them recess, remembering the exact spot in which they stood so they can return to it when they process.

He will explain the exact sequence and manner in which all members of the wedding party are to enter and leave the church sanctuary and will have them practice these movements. He will interpret to the ushers exactly what is expected of them and will also indicate to the bride's father how he fulfills his role in the wedding. He will also allow plenty of time for questions. The importance of the rehearsal to all participants is great, and you as the bridal couple should take it very seriously. Insist that all concerned must be present on time and must give careful attention to all directions they receive from the pastor.

THE WEDDING CEREMONY

The organist will begin to play appropriate music well in advance of the announced hour of the ceremony, and the ushers will also be on hand early to see to the cordial welcome of all guests. The "bride's side" is traditionally the left side as one faces the altar or communion table, and the "groom's side" is on the right. Sufficient seating should be reserved in the front pews on these respective sides for the immediate families and close relatives of the bride and groom. Other guests may be seated on the side of their choice, but it is not necessary for the usher to ask a guest, "Friend of the bride or friend of the groom?" He may word his question more tactfully, "Is there any particular location where you would like to sit?" If no preference is expressed, he will offer the best available seating on either side. In seating the guests, the ushers will escort each lady individually insofar as time permits. The ushers should recognize that they are the official hosts on behalf of the couple, and they should take the responsibility for doing everything possible to provide for the comfort of the guests. If attention needs to be given to such matters as lighting, ventilation, or heat, they should find the church sexton or the pastor and have appropriate action taken; or if necessary should do it themselves.

The seating of the mothers of the bride and groom is the signal that the service is about to begin. The groom's mother is escorted to her place in the front pew on the right-hand side, preferably by an usher who has some personal association with the groom's family.

Then the bride's mother is escorted to a place in the opposite pew by an usher who is associated with her family. Thereafter, no guests are seated by the ushers except perhaps inconspicuously using a side aisle.

As the organist begins playing the wedding march, the ushers two by two, followed by the bridesmaids, begin their journey down the aisle. The bridesmaids go one at a time, followed by the maid of honor, the flower girls, the ring bearer (if desired), and finally the bride. In the event that children are not included, the rings are carried by the best man and maid of honor. When the procession begins, the pastor, the best man, and the groom walk out unobtrusively from the front or side wing of the church to their place at the front.

The focal point of the processional then becomes the bride as she is escorted down the aisle on her father's right arm. If he is going to "give her away," he stops by the front pew and remains there until the time comes for his participation. If not, he takes his place quietly by his wife in the front pew.

The generally accepted wedding ritual among Protestants is the Anglican ceremony from the Episcopal *Book of Common Prayer*. This is adapted and modified in various denominations.[2] Pastors from the free-church traditions are more likely to take substantial liberties with the traditional service. They sometimes even allow the prospective bride and groom to work out their own variations, so long as these do not violate the spirit of the ceremony.

In most contemporary ceremonies the old promise of the bride to obey her husband has been left out, and in the light of today's mutuality this omission is a good one. Another contemporary innovation, sometimes, is the leaving out of the question, "Who giveth this woman to be married to this man?" The reason for this omission is that the father comes down the aisle with his daughter and by his actions gives her away, thus making unnecessary any words. The omission, of course, is optional.

There are other liberties which can be taken in the traditional service, depending upon one's philosophy and the permissiveness of the pastor and parents. You can add extra music and prayers, times of silence, the singing of hymns by the congregation, and even the repeating of one's own vows instead of the traditional "I will."[3]

The basic element which makes a wedding valid is the agreement between the two parties, or what Henry A. Bowman calls "consensus."[4] This is an action of decision on the part of the couple which publicly expresses itself when the minister questions both of them in words like these:

> Wilt thou have this Woman [Man] to thy wedded wife [husband], to live together after God's ordinance in the holy estate of Matrimony? Wilt thou love her [him], comfort her [him], honour, and keep her [him] in sickness and in health; and, forsaking all others, keep thee only unto her, so long as ye both shall live?[5]

Their answers of "I will" are the important words. These express the determination of these two people which (rather than any act of the state or church) constitutes the validity of marriage. The response of "I will" is not a mild consent. The bride and groom are implying (or should be): "With all the best in my personality, by a carefully considered and profound act of will, with full awareness of what I am doing, I will to have her [or him]."[6]

When each has made this important commitment, the question may then be asked, "Who gives this woman to be married to this man?" and the father replies, "Her mother and I do." He places his daughter's hand in the outstretched hand of the groom and sits down. At this point the bride gives her flowers to the maid of honor and has her veil lifted.

After the vows of marriage have been taken (or repeated to each other), the pastor will instruct the couple to join their hands together. He may say something like this to them:

> The marriage vows which you have made this day are voluntary and equal, the same for the man as for the woman. Regard them not as burdens to weigh you down, but as winged hopes and promises to bear you up to a more abundant life. Remember that true love is not the passion to possess and rule, but the desire to give, and to share, and to bless. Let no secret divide, no rivalry estrange, and no difference embitter your hearts, but seek by openness, reason, and goodwill to find the spiritual key of peace. Be not elated by prosperity, nor overcome by adversity, but study to be open with one another and have a firm faith in God.

Not only these words, but the clasping of their right hands together will be a token of their oneness as they in marriage will join their bodies together. This part of the ceremony, together with the kiss of benediction, has a deep symbolic meaning of their bond of love.

The final act of the ceremony is the pastor's announcement to the assembled congregation that the couple are now husband and wife, followed by the words: "Those whom God has truly joined together no man can put asunder."

The ceremony ends with the benediction or blessing. It is optional whether the newly married couple will kneel for this prayer. The traditions of the church will probably prevail in this matter.

Following the benediction the ceremony is sealed by the exchange of the "holy kiss" and the bride's flowers are returned to her. Then the bride and groom, walking arm in arm and followed by their entourage, go back down the aisle to the sprightly strains of the recessional wedding music.[7]

When the party has left the sanctuary, the ushers will escort the close relatives out. They are to reverse the entry pattern: The bride's mother is escorted out first, followed by the father. Next, the groom's mother and father. As soon as they are out, one of the ushers will go down front and announce to all assembled, "Other guests may now be excused."

THE RECEPTION

It is official! You are now "Mr. and Mrs." and your friends and family will want to congratulate you. As soon as possible after the wedding ceremony, when the pictures in the church have been taken and the marriage license has been signed, you will want to go promptly to the reception. When you arrive at the designated place (be it church parlor, bride's home, or hotel suite) you will want to organize the reception line promptly, as guests will be eagerly waiting.[8] Be considerate of your guests and do not make them wait for the taking of further pictures. This can be done later.

The keynote of the reception should be simplicity. You do not need a lavish display. Remember that *you* are the reason people come to your reception. If your wedding is held in the warm months of the year, garden flowers can be much in evidence as decoration. If it is wintertime, however, why not plan to have someone bring to the reception the flowers that were used in the church sanctuary?

If your wedding is an afternoon affair, the reception may include a dinner. Economy may dictate having only the immediate families present.[9] If no meal is desired, the wedding cake is placed on a buffet or table which is draped with a white cloth and backed by a centerpiece of white flowers. At a small reception the cake can be a fruit cake; otherwise it is usually a white pound cake with appropriate decorations. The bride always cuts the first piece, sharing it with the groom.

When it comes time to leave, the bride will want to throw her bouquet to her bridesmaids or other friends. It is great fun to see who catches it, for it is said that she will be the next to marry! After the two of you have changed into travel clothes you will go out to your car amid the hail of rice and bid your good-byes. You are off to the new and thrilling adventure of marriage!

My darling, my bride,
*   We are deliciously married.*
I want to consume you.

You are totally and completely mine,
*   Yet, as I look at you,*
I confess that I honestly don't know you,
*   And I am afraid.*

My sweetheart, my own,
*   You are to me as a mountain of meaning.*
I want to scale the summit now,
*   But I only can take one step.*

My darling, my sweet bride,
*   Our love is a precious fire.*
Let us feed it patiently.

7

A Purposeful Interlude

AN ARTIST CAREFULLY AND PAINSTAKINGLY WORKS on some minute details of his painting. He stands close to his canvas and works on it for what seems like a long time, but then he steps back in order to get a better perspective. This is the purpose of a honeymoon: to step back after the exciting days of the wedding in order to get life back in focus. The honeymoon is an interlude between courtship and marriage.

Where should you go for your honeymoon? How long should you stay? These important questions should be carefully considered and decided long before the wedding. Getting married is something like piloting a large ocean liner. When a great ship is going at top speed, it needs a mile to come to a stop, so the captain has to plan at least a mile ahead. Your "mile ahead" in planning for your honeymoon may actually be several months, because if you are going to a hotel or are renting a cabin at a resort, you may have to make your reservation far in advance.

Where should you go? The world is at your doorway. With cars, buses, ships, trains, and jets, there are very few limitations. Time and finances, rather than distances, will determine your destination. Plan a leisurely honeymoon, however, for it cannot be a truly purposeful interlude in your lives if you are involved in a hectic and wearying schedule of travel. Ambitious trips are likely to begin with enthusiasm and end with fatigue, if not total exhaustion—the very opposite of what you want to achieve. The important emphasis is *leisureliness*. It is best if you do not have to punch any timeclocks or meet any deadlines. Have you thought about some quiet, secluded spot which is not far away from home, but where you will not be disturbed?

One precaution: Make sure you know what you are doing before you venture off to certain kinds of activities. One couple on the advice of a friend spent their honeymoon at a lovely Arizona dude ranch. Beautiful, exotic, exciting, but the poor bride had never before ridden horseback! So, in addition to the complex problems of marital adjustment, she had difficulty sitting down after the first day on the trail. Imagine a bride on her honeymoon with saddlesores!

The two of you will want to have the opportunity to be alone together in a relaxed environment, to get to know each other in a new and deeper way, and to enjoy one another before you have to return home and take up the tasks of housekeeping and earning a living. You may have done a marvelous job planning and carrying out all the details of your wedding, and things may have gone off smoothly, but the experience has been fatiguing and you both are more tired emotionally and physically than you may realize. You need this chance to relax and to replenish your physical and spiritual resources.

One of the tasks of the honeymoon interlude is to become acquainted with one another. In the courtship days you talked and probed each other's minds and personalities. You liked what you found. You dated and wrote letters and were refreshing to one another, and so you wanted to be together for always. Now your dream has become a reality. This is not a "happy ending," but a beginning, a thrilling and exciting commencement. In many respects an individual resembles an iceberg in that much of what he really is as a person lies beneath the surface. Therefore these will be days of probing and penetrating the hidden facets of each other's personalities. The experience will be fascinating, but it will also be nerve-racking, for you will find subtleties in your loved one's inner being which you never before knew existed. These will range all the way from the superficial discovery that you have married "a fresh-air fiend who wants the window wide open every night" to the deep mysteries of knowing each other through physical oneness.

Although in chapter nine we will be dealing in more detail with the subject of sex in marriage, a word ought to be said now about your first experience of intimacy. Much depends upon your mental attitude and how physically exhausted you both may be from the rigors of the wedding. In order to recover physically and mentally from this fatigue, some thoughtful husbands have even suggested that the first act of sex be put off until both have had a good night's rest. Whatever you decide, all your dealings with one another ought to be characterized by gentleness and understanding. A wedding bed is no place for aggressive self-assertion or harmful force. The key is found in 1 Corinthians 13: "Love is patient and kind . . . is not arrogant or rude."

Many a marriage has been seriously marred by thoughtlessly allowing animal passion to take over. Remember that intercourse is not just a fusion of bodies, but a delicate intermingling of the totality of two persons—heart, mind, soul, and strength. There are few if any experiences in this world that even come close to the breathtaking ecstasy of the sexual intimacy of husband and wife. It is the outward manifestation of the biblical phrase "one flesh." Achieving a good sex adjustment is far from automatic. The marriage experts tell us that more than half of all newlyweds fail to attain complete sexual harmony during the honeymoon, so don't be apprehensive if your adjustment is slow. Whether or not you are able to attain complete oneness depends on many hard-to-describe factors, but your honeymoon should provide you with the kind of setting and atmosphere to aid you both in making the right beginning.

Wherever you are, you will have the heavenly feeling of doing things and going places together in a new and different framework. You may undergo the sensation of being newly created, "born all over again." It is no accident, therefore, that the apostle Paul used marriage as the analogy to describe the "new life in Christ." When the Christian believer has united himself to God and through an act of commitment has consciously tried to bring the spirit of Jesus into his life, there occurs a mystical union very much like that of the uniting of two loved ones in marriage. Union with Christ results in "new life" (a new perspective toward life and other persons, a new set of values which are "Christ-centered"). In marriage you experience some (not all) of this "new life" as you have your first sexual relationship, your first meal together, your first church service as man and wife. Never again will you be the same; you are and will forevermore be different because of your life together. As you revel in this delicious new feeling, remember the words of the Scriptures: "This is the day which the Lord has made; let us rejoice and be glad in it" (Psalm 118:24).

Do not worry if you feel a little self-conscious on your honeymoon when you meet strangers. It is only natural. All newlyweds seem to feel as if the eyes of the world are upon them, but they really are not. It is just that you need time to get used to your new role. Maybe you will have an experience like that of another married couple on their honeymoon:

> When we drove up to the Norwich Inn, we were determined to act so calmly and naturally that no one would know we'd just gotten married. Jan went in first to pick up the reservations and I followed after with the suitcases. Despite my efforts to appear blasé, the guests in the lobby seemed to be looking at me and nodding their heads knowingly. While I was disconcertedly trying to figure out how they guessed our secret, Jan turned around and burst out laughing. I had perched one of her little hats on my head while unloading the trunk and it was still there![1]

Amusing incidents such as this will give you cause for recalling your honeymoon experiences with nostalgia for years to come.

Another important question to be considered is: How much will our interlude cost? The groom is responsible for paying the expenses of the honeymoon, and unless he has received a substantial gift from family or relatives, money will be a limiting factor—especially if one or both is still in school!

Some marriage counselors recommend a honeymoon of splurging, but the cost must be measured against the budget for the other 51 weeks of the year. It does not make sense to mortgage the future to pay for one week of living it up; marriage has enough built-in problems without adding others. One couple solved the financial problem by offering to keep house for a family in New Jersey who were going to Florida for two weeks. This arrangement gave them the privacy they needed plus access to New York City, where they took in a Broadway show and made several leisurely trips to the Metropolitan Museum of Art.

As each of you reveals more and more of your true self to the other, unexpected qualities are bound to emerge—some that you will like and others which will prove disappointing. After all, how can two individuals with two separate pairs of parents and two differing backgrounds *not* have personality differences? However, the wise and mature mate, deeply committed to his beloved, will accept these differences and adjust to the other in love. A famous marriage expert summarizes what we have been trying to communicate:

What makes a honeymoon a honeymoon is not expensive hotels, or a shiny new roadster, or a breath-taking trousseau. What makes a honeymoon is a deep feeling of love in the hearts of two people who swim, read, hear the wood thrush at dusk, walk down a country road as they establish a more intimate pattern of togetherness. The gift of love is a precious and delicate thing. . . . If the miracle of the honeymoon is to be maintained there must be a never-ending renewal of its joy in togetherness, and no taking each other for granted. Problems must be met together. . . . Perhaps after she has learned to make the coffee his way, he just drinks it without a word of appreciation. Then some morning when she is in the kitchen in curlers and an apron, streaked with absent-minded cooking, he will tell her how beautiful he thinks she is. . . . To have is passive, and is usually consummated on their wedding day, but to hold is active, and can never be quite finished so long as they live.[2]

Your life together has begun. Because of your honeymoon—your purposeful interlude—you have begun to walk down the road of life with a more confident step and a resolute spirit. You are on your journey of love together, "forsaking all others . . . so long as you both shall live."

The sands of time are running out;
The trap is set and just about
To spring on him and put to rout
All the joys of bachelorhood.
But let it please be understood:
A life with wife is very good.

8

Living Together:
A Partnership of Equals

THUS THE LITTLE POEM by Pat Cunningham sets the spirit of marriage. Marriage *is* good, because God made it that way. But because of the intimate nature of marriage and the fact that it involves fallible human beings who bring with them their insecurities and their personal identity problems, life together is anything but a romantic gift from Santa Claus. Marriage to be good must be thought of as a partnership of equals in which both persons work hard at contributing to each other an honest share of give and take, of endeavor and adjustment.

Two themes which run all through the melody of marriage are *union* and *freedom to be one's self.* The idea of union has already been touched on in this book. It is the legitimate and real concept of "one flesh." As a newly married couple you both begin to blend and bend into oneness. Psychologically and spiritually you cease to be two separate individuals and find yourselves drawn closer into a complete unity. This process takes time, like the coming together of the waters of the Missouri and Mississippi rivers, which run along within the same banks for several miles before they lose their identity.

The second and equally legitimate theme is that of freedom to be yourself. When you love another person and that person loves you in return, there is a wholeness, a completion. Being loved frees you to be yourself. Instead of emptiness, frustration, and unhappiness (which impel you to attempt to snatch from life those things that your hostility actually blocks), you are realized and able to be productive and creative; yes, you are able to be what God intended you to be. One writer put it this way: "Marriage is not so much a cement as it is a solvent, a freeing-up of this man and this woman to be themselves and to help each other in the process of self-discovery."[1]

Notice the word "process." It implies growth or a journey along a continuous course. Neither the unity nor the freedom of a couple is fully developed at the beginning stages of marriage. Like maturity, both of these are brought about by months and years of living together in an atmosphere of security and trust. In the Bible, the book of John, referring to the believer's relationship to his Lord, expresses this same concept: "If you abide in me, and my words abide in you, ask whatever you will and it shall be done for you" (John 15:7). The word "abide" is the crux of the matter. To abide means to live with, to settle down, to remain. Abiding is not a haphazard affair: it is a long-term proposition.

To create a happy Christian home you will have to become like a resourceful gardener. You will need a background of knowledge to draw upon if you are to know what things are necessary to enrich the soil. You will need the skill to prepare the seeds and plant them. You will need the patience to watch them grow and the faith that God will supply the proper elements conducive to growth. And you will need the gratitude to recognize when, partially from your efforts, the garden has matured and produced its fruits.

As a person matured and freed by your loved one's trust and affection you will be satisfied and fulfilled. You will not require outward rewards or recognition, because your inner self-image has been realized and you have been made to feel needed. There will be no reason for you to have feelings of inferiority; you can approach any task in the home, church, or world for the sheer joy of it without wearing your emotions on your sleeve or pouting if you do not get the proper reward.

This process in marriage is akin to the religious doctrine of justification by faith, which tells us that God's love grasps us and we are accepted by him. We are loved in spite of our unlovableness. We are approved. Being able to accept this acceptance from God frees us from trying to dominate other people to "prove" or "earn" our approval. Being justified (an ancient legal term used by Paul), we can love other people for what they are and not for what we can get from them. We are further freed from outward compulsion (the Law) to the law of love, which binds us ever closer to the needs in others as Jesus was bound.

"To bear one another's burdens," as we are directed in Galatians 6:2, is an impossibility unless we have first accepted the approving love of God. Likewise, God's love as it is embodied in your loved one is what frees you in marriage to be your best self. Paul wrote to his friend Timothy some words that make little sense unless you understand them from the above insight: "Do your best to present yourself to God as one approved, a workman who has no need to be ashamed, rightly handling the word of truth" (2 Timothy 2:15).

The knowledge of your acceptance is what frees you from your inner anxieties due to a faulty self-image. As you become united with your beloved and are aware of a mutual response, you also come to love yourself in the best sense, thus fulfilling a biblical insight which has baffled mankind for centuries. It was Jesus who said, "You shall love the Lord your God with all your heart, and with all your soul, and with all your strength, and with all your mind; and your neighbor *as yourself*" (Luke 10:27, italics mine).

Read what the psychiatrist, Erich Fromm, says about these words:

> The idea expressed in the Biblical "Love thy neighbor as thyself!" implies that respect for one's own integrity and uniqueness, love for and understanding of one's own self, cannot be separated from respect and love and understanding for another individual.[2]

To love others does not mean under any circumstances to hate yourself, or that if you love yourself it is a sin. No, the truth is that you cannot love others productively and responsibly unless you have also been freed by another's love to love yourself. This process begins, of course, in childhood with your relation to your mother and father, but it is brought to its apex when you leave your parents and transfer your love to your marriage mate. Many problems in marriage stem from the husband's or wife's parents who themselves did not have a good marital relationship and therefore were not able to love their children adequately. Maybe they used their love in a domineering way or used it as a threat, withholding it to insure obedience. This distortion of love (keeping it from maturing) is a serious problem. Most of the difficulties in marriage can be traced to an immature concept of the self, due to the distortion or lack of love.[3]

Such immaturity can lead, in some persons, to extremes of abnormal or seriously distorted personality behavior. As time goes on, if you discover that there are impasses in your relationships which worry you, these may be danger signals indicating that you need outside help. Your pastor or family physician can discuss these problems with you and direct you to the right kind of psychological or psychiatric counselors.

"We love because God first loved us," we are reminded in 1 John 4:19. This statement can be paraphrased in the light of the things we have been talking about. You can have the ability to give without exploiting, or "lording it over," or becoming excessively dependent on your mate, because God has blessed your union with life-giving love. As you grow into this realization of the grace of the marriage relationship, you will find an increasing mastery of your own human powers and will have the courage to rely on them, unperturbed about what others outside the family will think or say. Your home will be the place where you can be yourself and you can accept your mate and children as they are.

Having this center of security allows you to radiate outward, like the ever-widening concentric circles made by tossing a pebble into a pond. Being freed to love at home means you are also released to love and accept people who are outside the circle of your family without prejudice. A wonderful example of a mature father is found in Atticus Finch, in *To Kill a Mockingbird*. His daughter is speaking:

"Atticus," . . . "what exactly is a nigger-lover?"

Atticus's face was grave. "Has somebody been calling you that?"

"No sir, Mrs. Dubose calls you that. She warms up every afternoon calling you that. Francis called me that last Christmas, that's where I first heard it."

"Is that the reason you jumped on him?" asked Atticus.

"Yes sir. . . ."

"Then why are you asking me what it means?"

I tried to explain to Atticus that it wasn't so much what Francis said that had infuriated me as the way he had said it. "It was like he'd said snot-nose or somethin'."

"Scout," said Atticus, "nigger-lover is just one of those terms that don't mean anything—like snot-nose. It's hard to explain—ignorant, trashy people use it when they think somebody's favoring Negroes over and above themselves. It's slipped into usage with some people like ourselves, when they want a common, ugly term to label somebody."

"You aren't really a nigger-lover, then, are you?"

"I certainly am. I do my best to love everybody. . . . I'm hard put, sometimes—baby, it's never an insult to be called what somebody thinks is a bad name. It just shows you how poor that person is, it doesn't hurt you."[4]

Of course it didn't hurt Atticus, because he was secure within. And the rest of us can experience that same kind of security. With the knowledge that you are secure, three more elements of love become apparent. They are an active concern, a respect for, and a feeling of duty toward your partner.

To "bear one another's burdens" is the essence of an active care and concern. True love binds you to the needs of your loved one. As you grow in love you will be able to anticipate these needs (the melody of union drowns out separateness here). You become so close that you know your partner's every mood and are able to adjust to it— or sometimes you will be able, by saying the right word or doing a small loving act (for instance, rubbing the back during a menstrual period), to lift the mood. There will be times of sacrifice when your own wants and desires will have to be placed second (sublimated) or put aside because of illness or an accident. There are mountaintops and valleys in every marriage; as the writer of Job put it, "Man is born to trouble as the sparks fly upward" (Job 5:7). A deep concern makes allowances for these times. It manifests itself in patience. Mature love says with Jacob after he had worked seven years to earn the hand of Rachel: "They seemed to him but a few days because of the love he had for her" (Genesis 29:20).

Sometimes the dominant theme is separateness. There must be breathing room if love is to flourish and grow. A gardener prepares the soil and plants the seed and occasionally cultivates, but there are periods of time when he must step aside and allow the forces of nature to take over. So it is with your marriage. Concern for your loved one could easily become an overbearing and unhealthy possessiveness if it were not for the second manifestation of mature love: a respect for his rights as a person. You must never lose sight of one another as children of God. Each of you has a uniqueness of personality. There is a sacredness (an inherent God-given worth) which indwells everyone, and this quality must be respected. You both need *lebensraum,* room to develop your own potential. Time needs to be given to the other so that he can pursue his interests. You ought to encourage your mate's artistic or athletic abilities, his woodworking skills or her interest in sewing or weaving. When children come, the husband might well volunteer to spend a half a day or so each week taking over the responsibilities of the home so that the wife can get out. A mutual love frees each of you to respect each other, and respect involves trust and a regard for the other's privacy. Your mate should have personal areas of interest and even a personal allowance, be it ever so modest, to indulge in personal whims and fancies. Respect means that though you probably will be annoyed at times with your mate's petty faults (like being late), your commitment to his inner potential will allow you to endure these things and love him as he is and for what he is.

The third strand of the cord of affection is duty. Much of the distortion of what marriage means comes from a maudlin concept of romantic love. Love is much more than a thrilly feeling that makes delightful little squiggles run up and down the spine. This kind of nonsense soon dies, and if there is not a mature framework of understanding from which to operate, then the marriage dies also.

Duty does not come from the outside, but from within. It is the result of committing your life to your loved one as both of you entrust yourselves to the loving care of God, whose love responds to your need for security and fills you with confidence and inner peace. In spite of the outside threats and the ups and downs of everyday life with its hosts of problems, you can be of good cheer because you know through Christ that God has "overcome the world" (John 16:33). Duty comes as the result of the overflow of God's grace in your lives. In gratitude to God for bringing you two together, making you secure, and freeing you to love, you are willing and able to be responsible for each other. Response is the root meaning of duty. To be able to respond, therefore, is *not* to depend on emotion or on getting something for the other out of gratitude for the privilege of being loved.

Duty has other implications, too. It means faithfulness. It means literally the fulfillment of the vows that were made at the wedding in reply to the question, "Will you be true to him (her) in sickness and in health, in sorrow and in joy, forsaking all others as long as you both shall live?" The answer "I will" was your pledge in faith to a lifelong obligation, to an *un*limited liability. It means that no matter how much your circumstances might change, your love will remain constant. When children come, when illnesses strike, when the job dictates a change in living location or economic status, you will be standing by and your love can be counted on. Even when someone in your family may be undergoing an inner crisis, and be hard to live with and to love, your support will continue to undergird that person.

One of the best illustrations of this relationship is found in the Negro character "Mama," in Lorraine Hansberry's great drama *A Raisin in the Sun*. Mama has received a large sum of money from an insurance policy following her husband's death. Her son Walter has taken part of the money and placed a down payment on a house in a white suburb called Clybourne Park. The other half he has lost in a crooked business deal. A white man from the Clybourne Park Improvement Association has called to try and prevent them from moving in by offering them a bonus if they will sell the house. Much to the disgust of Mama and her daughter Beneatha, Walter now calls the man—presumably to tell him the family will accept the money. Beneatha snarls at Walter, denouncing him as something less than a man, but Mama becomes incensed and immediately defends him. She tells Beneatha that basic to the stability of a family is an underlying love for one another. Beneatha protests that her groveling brother is not worth loving. To this Mama gives a classic reply, telling Beneatha and the world that there is always something in a person left to love. The time when a person needs being loved the most, she says, is when he is beaten and is ready to give up.[5]

Mama's love is no fair-weather commitment. It is "for better or for worse." She knows that when a person is most miserable and has lost his self-esteem, this is the very time when he needs undergirding and support. "Love . . . endures all things. Love never ends" (1 Corinthians 13:7-8).

"If any man would come after me, let him deny himself and take up his cross and follow me" (Mark 8:34). Here in Jesus' words is the duty side of love. To take up your cross means to assume an obligation voluntarily. Often this is thought of in connection with some spectacular kind of action such as becoming a foreign missionary, but it is not necessarily so. To you, for example, it can mean sacrificial everyday duty to your family and neighbors. It can mean the taking-on of extra financial responsibilities for that new building fund at the church, or the giving-up of buying a new car so that Mary can go back to college and finish her education.

Togetherness and apartness, these are the two themes which are woven into the fabric of any happy marriage. The husband goes to work in the morning, leaving the wife to her household chores. Both have their individualities, their different parts to play. Then comes the evening and, with it, togetherness. When little things can be shared, like doing the dishes together, or helping to mark a skirt, or holding a ladder while a nail gets driven—these are the cords which tie you together. Then at close of day, when tired and weary you climb into bed, the act of love-making somehow catches up the total scope of your common existence. There is more than mere physical union; there is wholeness, completeness, satisfying and enduring oneness.

When side by side I focus on your face,
I am silently stirred, buoyed by your embrace.

We look into each other's eyes, two separate souls,
Tied together by commitments and common goals.

You come to me; I take you for my own;
There is completeness and I know as I am known.

From you I derive daring, a place in the sun;
We are mystically merged as the two become one.

We are side by side and I focus on your form;
We are two again, alive, vibrant, and warm.

9
The Sexual Side
of Love and Marriage

MARRIAGE WAS INSTITUTED BY THE CREATOR, in part for the purpose of continuing the human race. But man is more than an animal and he does not live "by bread alone." Deep within all normal human beings is an emptiness that yearns to be filled, a strong need for mutual belonging. This urge is as mysterious and as impossible of definition as the pull of the tides, yet it comes to almost everybody. It is a built-in attraction for the opposite sex, established by God, who himself termed it good.

The need for having some person of the opposite sex to complement and fulfill oneself as a person is well expressed by Robert Browning to his beloved Elizabeth Barrett in *The Barretts of Wimpole Street*. "Robert, for what have I to give you?" she asks. And he replies, "I tell you . . . that my need of you is as urgent as your need of me. If your weakness asks my strength for support, my abundant strength cries out for your weakness to complete my life and myself."[1] Here is the uniting of two personalities on the spiritual level.

A further dimension is attained when in the secure setting of marriage two people in love join in the physical uniting of their bodies. By this act they are able to gather up all of the experiences of their common life together and infuse them with new meaning. The work of the office, the struggle of housekeeping, the raising of children— all these become not just insignificant tasks, but sacramental parts of a high calling. Marriage thus becomes God's vehicle for transmitting his love to all mankind.

Sex plays a special part in the sharing of God's love. God transmits the meaning of love to us through other people, and uniquely through families. When a husband and wife manifest in their marital relations a humble faith in God and are renewed daily by an awareness of the indwelling Christ, they are able to fulfill each other in a way that overcomes their emptiness. Their mutual love gives them a confidence that they are accepted in life and have a belonging in eternity. This is the essence of salvation—and the beginning of maturity!

This religious dimension allows them to accept one another as persons and not "things." It frees them for creative living in the relaxed atmosphere of a home where both can develop their own personalities without domination. There is a mutual concern for one another and a striving for shared goals. When children are born, they enter the home able to grow amid a protecting environment of security. Parents who are secure in their own love can give to their children freedom to experiment, opportunities for self-expression, and the experience of realizing their God-given potential. Such ideal conditions do not *always* prevail, of course. In all families, at times tempers are lost, bad judgment is used, and disagreements occur. Nonetheless, at the center of the truly Christian family is a loving relationship, which makes all the difference. Love has a way of overcoming and compensating for human frailty and errors in judgment.

But what have we said, so far, about sex? Chiefly this: In married life, sex is not the be-all and end-all. It is but one of the many facets of the complex relationship between two people. It *is* important, but it needs to be seen in proper perspective, as a part of the total picture. It cannot be separated from the rest of marriage any more than the flour can be separated from all the rest of the ingredients of a cake. Everything in married life is interrelated and affects everything else.

To try to isolate sex from other aspects of life is to make it dreadfully artificial—if not false.

This same mistake was made by the Church Fathers many centuries ago when they tried to separate man into two parts: a body and a soul. They placed the higher value on the soul and said that the body was a "prison house" from which the soul should be liberated. As a result of this false interpretation, the church regarded sex as a regrettable and unmentionable necessity. Before the Reformation, sexual asceticism was considered one of the primary aims of the good life, and even the great fourth-century saint Augustine wrote that "those who are virgins are more pleasing in God's sight and will have greater reward in heaven."

Thank goodness, biblical scholars have corrected this misinterpretation. They have carefully restudied the biblical material and have shown conclusively that the Fall of Man cannot be correctly interpreted in sexual terms but rather as a result of man's pride and rebellion. Furthermore, they have recognized that the Bible, especially the creation story, does not sanction a male-dominated society. The writers of Genesis were concerned only with the problem of sin and evil, a matter that still concerns us all very deeply. However, the truth that frees mankind is the fact that the world is still God's and he continues to love it!

The good news of the gospel is that mankind has been redeemed and the Fall described in Genesis has been overcome. God's suffering love in Jesus Christ has personally come into the world and made it possible for men and women to be liberated from their false selves. The embodiment of this love is seen in the cross, the supreme length to which God would go in offering his grace to man. It is this same suffering love of God which comes to man supremely in man's marital and family relations.

The mistake being made today is the opposite error from that of the early churchmen. It is the glorifying of the body apart from the rest of man's capacities. In our culture, sex has become an entity by itself, and this has seeped into the literature of marriage. Writers too often treat the act of sexual intercourse mechanistically and in isolation. A happy marriage is *not* the result of adequate sexual technique. If it were so, then prostitutes would probably make the best wives! A happy marriage is one which is based on a mature love. Psychiatrist Erich Fromm's words may be helpful here:

> Love is not the result of adequate sexual satisfaction, but sexual happiness . . . is the result of love. . . . The study of the most frequent sexual problems—frigidity in women, and the more or less severe forms of psychic impotence in men—shows that the cause does not lie in a lack of knowledge of the right technique, but in the inhibitions which make it impossible to love. . . . If a sexually inhibited person can emerge from fear or hate, and hence become capable of loving, his or her sexual problems are solved. If not, no amount of knowledge about sexual techniques will help.[2]

Man does not consist of a tomb-like body from which his soul must be set free; nor, on the other hand, of a body in isolation from a soul. The sexual function is part of the whole person, not an independent element. The truth is found in the Hebrew word *nephesh,* which refers to the whole of a human being and pictures him as a unity of body *and* soul, inextricably related. Marriage, therefore, is the blending of two personalities each consisting of body and soul, and the sex relationship in marriage is a personal act which affects the whole being. For this reason two people are able to make their physical union creative as well as procreative.

It is the communication function of sex which needs further exploration. The word "intercourse" means "communion." It also means "knowing," like the Hebrew word *yada:* "Cain knew his wife, and she conceived and bore Enoch" (Genesis 4:17). In the act of intercourse you will be able to exchange a kind of knowledge with your partner which can be given in no other way. This knowledge is not objective information, but personal understanding. We are able to experience a sense of fulfillment, of grace, of being given a gift we did not earn. Our emptiness becomes filled with ecstatic peace and well being. There is a release of built-up tension where understandable anxieties have been created due to the uncertainties and insecurities of life. True sexual love is the most perfect illustration of the biblical paradox that in giving we get and in losing we save. The sex act between two people who tenderly trust and love each other can be a means of communion as each gives to the other something of the strength of himself and in return receives a renewed self-assurance. The poet puts it in the following free verse:

> *I love you,*
> *Not only for what you are,*
> *But for what I am*
> *When I am with you.*
> *I love you,*
> *Not only for what*
> *You have made of yourself,*
> *But for what*
> *You are making of me.*
> *I love you*
> *For the part of me*
> *That you bring out;*
> *I love you*
> *For putting your hand*
> *Into my heaped-up heart*
> *And passing over*
> *All the foolish, weak things*
> *That you can't help*
> *Dimly seeing there,*
> *And for drawing out*
> *Into the light*
> *All the beautiful belongings*
> *That no one else had looked*
> *Quite far enough to find.*
> *I love you because you*
> *Are helping me to make*
> *Of the lumber of my life*
> *Not a tavern*
> *But a temple;*
> *Out of the works*
> *Of my every day*
> *Not a reproach*
> *But a song. . . .*[3]

The communication function of sex can be corrupted, as can all other aspects of life. One person may "use" the other as a means of merely satisfying selfish lusts. Because the magnetic pull of the sex urge is often so all-powerful and consuming, much care must be exercised to avoid lapsing into sin. The height of sexual sin is to treat another person as a "thing." We must remember that the marriage vows are not a blank check which permits sex-feelings to run rampant. A contemporary writer suggests that sex, like hand and mouth, must progress beyond the primary function. The mouth, while primarily an eating utensil, is also an organ of speech. The hand is primarily given as a claw, but it is also an instrument of writing and building. The function of sex is procreation, but only the poorest excuse for a human will crudely use it as a means of relief without entering into the creative delights of a mutual person-to-person relationship in communication.[4]

True love liberates us, but it does not free us to do what we please. Love that is Christian is a love which seeks to please those whom we love. We are called by God to be like Christ toward our neighbor (Matthew 22:39), and our closest neighbor is always our marriage-mate. Christlikeness in a specific situation may dictate that we exercise restraint and self-control. "For everything there is a season, and a time for every matter under heaven: . . . a time to embrace, and a time to refrain from embracing" (Ecclesiastes 3:1, 5). Love in marriage always involves thoughtfulness, understanding, and careful consideration for the other's feelings.

Let us now consider briefly some of the problems with which you may be confronted in the sexual realm of your marriage. In the early months there undoubtedly will be a period of getting adjusted. Psychologically speaking, we are conditioned by a culture and a view of life which says that sex must be withheld until after marriage. When marriage becomes a reality, many husbands and wives do not find it easy to put aside the inner restraints about sex which they have had from youth. It is somewhat difficult to make the transition from inhibition to responsiveness, especially on the part of the woman. However, with a permissive and patient partner, your sexual responsiveness will increase steadily.

Love-making is an art, and like all artistic endeavors it requires practice. Words are important because they provide the emotional context which sets the tone for responsiveness. One wise person has said that a person who wants to have a happy marriage should find a thousand ways to say "you are wonderful!"

You will want to keep up your personal attractiveness, for it is true that "cleanliness is next to godliness." Maintain the lines of communication at all times, for if these break down, so will your relationship. There must be honesty and frankness between you both, and these are difficult to achieve at the beginning of marriage. Tell each other of your inner feelings and desires. Lovemaking is a shared art which requires patience, thoughtfulness, perseverance, and above all a willingness to experiment.

Do not expect to achieve perfection overnight. It takes time. In any aspect of living you will have failures and you must expect them. One of the best illustrations of failing was the "Sultan of Swat," Babe Ruth, considered by most baseball experts as the greatest hitter of all time. He hit more home runs than anyone else in the history of the game, 851. *And yet Babe Ruth also struck out a record 1,330 times.* He learned through his experiences of failure, and so can you. Keep trying.

It is generally agreed that a woman's ability to respond to sexual stimulation is slower and more diffused than a man's. Most men are more readily excited sexually than women. Individuals differ, however, and this generalization does not necessarily apply to all couples. As time goes on, you will find out what is "right" for you. Dr. Floyd Martinson points up the basic principle when he writes:

It is generally agreed today that there are no right techniques for bringing about sex satisfaction, no right bodily positions of the partners in relation to each other, no right time of the day for love-making, and no right frequency of sex experience. Each is to be determined by the couple in respect for their mutual desires and wishes.[5]

The climax of love-play is the orgasm. This ecstasy of delight occurs when two people achieve a throbbing, tingling sensation together. It does not always happen, and (contrary to what you may have read) failure to experience it will not necessarily leave the woman with upset emotions or bodily fatigue. If the wife fails to reach an orgasm, she can nevertheless find her satisfaction in knowing that she has contributed to her mate's pleasure. One marriage expert has explained the woman's reaction this way:

> What the woman enjoys essentially is the man's eager pursuit of the pleasure he gains by possessing her. Freely giving her body to the man of her choice is an exciting experience for her, playing an important part in awakening her own desire. There is probably a parallel here with her maternal function in offering her breasts to her child. Her fulfillment is bound up with her awareness that she is meeting an urgent hunger in one she deeply loves.[6]

When the climax of your coitus has been reached, it is followed by a time of "afterglow" in which, peacefully relaxing in each other's arms, you experience the slow ebb of satisfying reverie and drift off into a refreshing sleep. Here again is the ever-recurring theme of union and separation, togetherness and apartness, but always with the mutual knowledge that your love is rooted and grounded in the divine Love which is the same yesterday, today, and forever "The eternal God is your dwelling place and underneath are the everlasting arms" (Deuteronomy 33:27).

As the years pass by and children come into your home, your sexual experiences will mature and deepen, reflecting the changes you will undergo. With the increasing responsibilities of parental and community pressures, you may yearn for the past, but no return is possible. Anne Morrow Lindbergh, in her little classic called *Gift from the Sea,* compares various seashells to the complexities of change within married life:

> One learns to accept the fact that no permanent return is possible to an old form of relationship; and, more deeply still, that there is no holding of a relationship to a single form. This is not tragedy but part of the ever-recurrent miracle of life and growth. All living relationships are in process of change, of expansion, and must perpetually be building themselves new forms. But there is no single fixed form to express such a changing relationship. There are perhaps different forms for each successive stage. . . .[7]

Mrs. Lindbergh goes on to say that when you love someone, you do not love that person in exactly the same way all the time, even though you might desire to do so. People have too little faith in the ebb and flow of their love relationship, she adds. They are afraid of change; they insist on the same old patterns when the only kind of lasting love relationships are characterized by "growth, in fluidity—in freedom, in the sense that the dancers are free, barely touching as they pass, but partners in the same pattern."[8]

One item remains for discussion: What about birth control? Contraception in a world of population explosion is a burning issue which needs serious consideration. Dr. John Rock, a noted Roman Catholic gynecologist, has written that birth control measures are a critical necessity. He says that more than half of the world goes to bed hungry every night and that we may have reached the most serious crisis in the history of mankind, for the growth rate is as urgent a problem as nuclear energy.[9] In the face of this deluge of humanity, science has developed a variety of new devices for controlling conception: pills, inexpensive foam packed in aerosol containers, plastic coils, and injections which prevent fertilization.

With the scientific ability now available to prevent the birth of unwanted millions in this country and abroad, it is the church—of all groups—that has dragged its feet. Specifically, the Roman Catholic Church has opposed the dissemination, sale, use, and prescription of artificial contraceptives. Many Protestant denominations, on the other hand, have come out in favor of their use. Here is an official Lutheran statement:

> God has established the sexual relation for the purpose of bringing husband and wife into full unity so that they may enrich and be a blessing to each other. . . . Husband and wife are called to exercise the power of procreation responsibly before God. This implies planning their parenthood in accordance with their ability to provide for their children and carefully nurture them in fullness of Christian faith and life. . . . Irresponsible conception of children up to the limit of biological capacity and selfish limitation of the number of children are equally detrimental. Choice as to means of conception control should be made upon professional medical advice.[10]

It is time to state a Protestant rationale for birth control, and there is a biblical basis for such a statement. It is the principle of "accountability to God" based on 1 Corinthians 10:31, "Whatever you do, do all to the glory of God." In order to receive God's blessing and reward more thankfully, married couples should plan and regulate the effects of their sexual activity with the help of contraceptives so that children who are produced will be desired both for themselves and for the time of their birth. God has endowed us all with brains and he expects us to use them. To bring children into the world irresponsibly without the resources to care for them adequately is selfish and sinful. Furthermore, to have the children realize they are unwanted burdens will seriously hamper their emotional security and probably warp their personalities for life.

Inasmuch as a healthy woman is capable of producing more than twenty children during her childbearing period, we must take into account what this potential means economically and physically. Entirely apart from the effect on the children, it is not good physically for a mother to bear a child every nine months. Such a routine depletes her psychic as well as her physical resources and energies. Medical experts suggest that at least two years ought to elapse between childbirths for the mother's optimal health. Furthermore, with the mounting cost of food, housing, and education, one needs to consider carefully to be sure that each child brought into the world will have the necessary resources for growing and maturing. Those parents who fail to exercise prudent stewardship of human life may be found wanting when they stand in judgment before God. Jesus said, "Truly, I say to you, as you did it to one of the least of these my brethren, you did it to me" (Matthew 25:40). The Quakers have said:

> Philadelphia Yearly Meeting of the Religious Society of Friends gladly accepts family life as a primary and sacred relationship. This responsibility and privilege is based on spiritual, physical and economic foundations. We believe that the quality of family life is enriched if each child can be wholeheartedly welcomed. Moreover, problems of poverty and emotional strain might be lessened if children were not born in too close succession nor too great numbers in relation to circumstances. We therefore endorse planned parenthood and hope that qualified professional advice may be given to those seeking it, concerning both contraception and the promotion of fertility when that is the need. Such planning contributes to the welfare not only of particular families, but of the nation and the world.[11]

Said Mary to John,
"Oh how you put on.
I don't like your taste
Of vanilla tooth paste.
And since I know what's best,
'Cause I've given it the test,
You'd better give in,
For I need to win."

Cried John to Mary,
"I'm really quite wary.
Since I had a sign, Ma'am,
That God's will is mine, Ma'am,
Let all men agree,
With Jehovah and me,
That chocolate brand,
Is where, Ma'am, I stand."

And each drew his rifle
Because of a trifle.[1]

10
Troubles or Trifles?

WARS IN MARRIAGE ARE COMMON. When two people live together, especially a young couple starting out in a cramped apartment or in a rented room, it is only natural and normal that differences will develop. Why wouldn't they? The husband and wife come from two different backgrounds with differing degrees of wants and tastes. She wants vanilla and he wants chocolate tooth paste. She squeezes the tube from the top, while he methodically rolls it from the bottom. To this little "love nest" they both bring their frustrations, their anxieties, and their hostilities. The miracle is not that they quarrel, but that quarrels do not happen more often. The man who brags, "My wife and I have not had one quarrel in twenty-five years," is either a liar or married to a vegetable!

The great mirage of romantic love is: "And they lived happily ever after." That statement may be true of fairy-tale characters but not of flesh-and-blood people. Marriage-mates live in close proximity with one another where they have both the marvelous possibility of creating community and the sobering hazard of conflict. Therefore it will be helpful for you to understand why troubles occur and to realize that your situation is not unique if there are problems in your marriage.

Many people report that one of the very first adjustments they have to make to married life is to come to terms with their deep-seated resentment at the loss of independence. The wife may be especially troubled in this way if she was working prior to the wedding. And resentment grows with fatigue. As one person has sarcastically said, it is a big comedown from moonlight and roses to daylight and dishes.

Money matters are another source of friction. Most marriage counselors rate the handling of finances as one of the top causes for marital strife. Two people bring with them vastly differing patterns of ideas and past habits about the meaning, value, and use of money. No matter how much a couple discuss finances before marriage, differences are apt to arise when they actually get right down to spending the family income. For instance, you and your mate may have agreed on certain good financial objectives during your period of engagement, but actual experience works out differently. One of you may be a very precise person while the other may not; one may be practical and "down-to-earth," the other flighty and emotional. What happens when the bank account is overdrawn? How do you pay for the non-budgeted TV set impulsively bought on credit? How about the wife's splurges for clothing? The financial battle lines are easily drawn, and the stage is set for marital war!

Doing things differently from the way in which you were brought up is another sensitive area where trouble can start. If all you hear from your partner are statements like "At our home we always had our Thanksgiving dinner at night," or "My family always opened their Christmas presents Christmas Eve," or "Daddy always brought Mother a rose on Valentine's day," then reaction and rebellion are bound to come. Sometimes, in fact, it will be accompanied by a thunderclap reply, "We do not have to do things in the same way as *your* folks did." And this is true. You as a new family will want to develop certain traditions of your own. An overdependence on either the husband's or wife's parents and their patterns is a sure way to trouble. You will have to help one another to make a "declaration of independence" from your respective families, and this is surely biblical.

Many times, troubles at home are the indirect result of hostility and frustrations from the outside world. A husband who has to cope with a neurotic foreman at the plant all day is bound to come home irritable and upset, at least sometimes. A wife who has been shopping all day or has attended a particularly fatiguing Settlement House board meeting is bound to bring some of her tiredness home with her. Being human, both will inadvertently heap hostile feelings upon the other. Furthermore, if both are "charged up" enough, the sparks will fly!

Television is a wonderful medium for bringing world events, sports contests, and drama into the home, but it also can be a complicating factor in marriage. Who watches which programs? When to turn it off? Many an argument gets started by an irate wife who says to her husband, "You never help me with the dishes anymore. All you ever do is sit by that TV set and watch whatever comes on. We never talk or think or read since we bought that thing." And he replies, "Aw, stop nagging. I've had a hard day at the office."

Most problems begin when people are tired. In spite of all our modern conveniences and gadgets, we tend to live at too fast a pace. We become worn out from rushing here and there trying to fulfill our domestic, civic, political, and social obligations. When exhausted, we allow little things to get on our nerves and become thoughtless and careless of our manner of speech. A word of criticism, harmlessly intended, is blown up all out of proportion, the spouse fights back, and trifles have grown into real trouble!

A Christian home is one where two people have dedicated themselves to the Christlike way and spirit. But growth takes time; nobody becomes a mature Christian all at once. Furthermore, the fact that one is a Christian does not mean that he (or she) is a perfect lover either, for no one is always loving or always lovable. A Christian in marriage therefore commits himself to the proposition that no amount of trouble is insurmountable. He will seek out and use some of the many resources that are always available for learning to keep differences in manageable proportions.

Bear in mind that mere differences of opinion are not at all the same thing as the tragic loss of emotional unity. In fact, differences of opinion can be quite creative, for these can help both partners to grow. They can mean both persons are maintaining their individuality and their ability to think for themselves. The husband may be fond of popular music, for example, while the wife may prefer the classics. At the beginning of their marriage this difference may be a petty source of irritation, especially if they live in a one-room apartment. In time, however, they can learn to respect the values of both kinds of musical expression while deepening their appreciation for each other's choice.

"Letting off steam" is not necessarily bad if both partners do not allow their emotional blowoffs to collide. Released emotional tension can be very therapeutic. As long as there is a background of commitment, security, and love, a verbal unwinding can be good. Actually, the home is the one place in the world where a person can "let down his hair" and can be himself, knowing that he will be accepted. The home's primary function is to be a cushion where the shocks and hurts of life are absorbed and perspective and courage are renewed.

How do two mature people handle normal marital troubles? First of all, both must face them squarely. If you are having differences, do not ignore them. Do not put your heads in the sand ostrich-fashion and expect them to go away, for they will not. You may succeed in arriving at an armed truce, but who wants to live in a state of quiet desperation? Take one problem at a time. Do not go off on tangents. If you are talking about a problem of the budgeting of money, stick to the subject and do not begin attacking your partner's family or basic honesty. Attack problems, not persons.

Probably the single most important ingredient in handling marital hurts is the ability to discuss them openly and intelligently. Talking about differences helps to let pent-up feelings get out into the open. As soon as emotions can be controlled, the problem at hand can be dealt with by asking, "How can *we* arrive at the amicable solution?" (Not "How am I going to get what I want?") The loving solution to any problem is not "all or nothing." In *To Kill a Mockingbird* Atticus Finch and his daughter Scout are discussing a school matter. Atticus asks, "Do you know what a compromise is?" Scout replies with a question: "Bending the law?" "No," says Atticus, "an agreement reached by mutual concessions."[2] In the calm of discussion an agreement is sure to be worked out by mutual concession, involving some give-and-take by both parties. The important word when arguments arise is *patience*. Wisdom is always on the side of the tortoise.

Some complex problems require many hours of thoughtful deliberation. The question of whether to buy a house, for instance, cannot be settled in a hurry. Many tense moments can be precipitated by arguments having to do with styles of architecture, location, finance, and plans for future family. These misunderstandings can simmer and boil over if they are not dealt with. Perhaps the most widespread cause of real trouble is the persistence of unresolved tensions. Always keep the channels of communication open; do not procrastinate. If possible, never go to sleep without reaffirming your basic love and loyalty to one another. If you can follow these general suggestions within the framework of your own individual intellectual and emotional make-up, most of your marital wounds can be healed, and year by year you will be growing closer together in Christian understanding and oneness.

There is every reason to believe that with a little patience, persistence, goodwill, and forgiving love you will be able to smooth over most normal problems. However, if you find that the issue is greater than what you think you can handle, you may need outside help. Many people turn to a mutual friend or neighbor for help. If this person is wise and mature, he may be of inestimable value. The one great danger here is a possibility that the friendship may be marred when and if the third party appears to side with one of the marriage partners against the other. Therefore if you find your marriage relationship in deep water, it would be wise to turn to a professional consultant such as a psychiatrist, a marriage counselor, or your pastor.

Troubles are generally trifles blown up. The best time to prevent a quarrel is before it starts, by creating an emotional climate where trifles can be kept small. Two time-proven ways of promoting a quarrel-free environment in the home are humor and a willingness to listen.

Try to make each other laugh every day if possible. A good sense of humor can lift your spirits by draining hostile feelings and relieving bottled-up tension. Everyday living gets pretty grim at times, and there are occasions when you might as well laugh as cry. Each husband-and-wife team should have their own little private jokes and funny expressions which only they can share. In one home there is a standing joke that always gets a guffaw. The wife uses a colloquial expression in regard to the serving of a meal. Right before dinner is ready she announces, "Come, everybody, supper is ready to be taken up." The husband good naturedly then begins to herd the children toward the stairs, winking and telling them to go on upstairs so mother can "take it up." She always looks half exasperated but manages a smile while the whole family roars! Trouble has a difficult time in that kind of atmosphere.

The art of creative listening is equally important. A wife can become a real artist at this point. One encourages her husband when he comes home at night to sit down immediately and unburden himself. Another waits until her husband's stomach is filled and then listens to the day's exploits and disasters. Each is sensitive to her husband's needs. And, likewise, an understanding husband can recognize that there are times when he needs to listen sympathetically to an account of the problems his wife is facing. Either partner can, by being skillful enough and by asking just the right questions, make it possible for the other to express his real self.

Creative listening is not passive but active; it communicates feelings of acceptance and need. It encourages the other person to analyze his own feelings and, miracle of miracles, to listen to himself. Creative listening involves empathy, the skill of being able to get into another person's skin, to discover his underlying motives, his emotional hungers. A little child was sent on an errand and was gone longer than her mother thought proper. When she returned and was asked for an explanation, she said, "I met Mary and her doll was broken, so I stopped to help her." "You mean you helped her fix the doll?" her mother asked. "No," said the little girl, "I stopped to help her cry." Creative listening is to weep sincerely with your mate when he has been hurt, to enter into his pain and frustration, to penetrate his loneliness at its deepest level. As you share one another's joys and woes, power is released. Trouble has no opportunity to develop in this kind of environment.

In addition to humor and creative listening as tension-relievers, there are a trio of B's that do not sting. These are necessary attributes which help add pleasure to home life. The first is BE ACCEPTING. A mature person is first of all a realist. He knows and unhesitantly accepts the fact that no one is perfect. Furthermore, he permits no deceiving of himself or anyone else. In this context, he realizes that life is not a bed of roses and neither is marriage. It is a process of trying and failing and trying again. He knows that in any satisfying relationship one must learn to live with faults, adjust to them, and love the virtues of the other person. Since he does not expect perfection, he is more able to go the second mile in being tolerant. Being accepting means, for example, that the husband who knows from experience that his wife gets increasingly tense and irritable a few days before her menstrual period will therefore be more restrained and tender toward her at that time. And the wife will recognize that her husband finds it harder to be charming when things are going badly on the job. Thus each learns to take the other's moodiness into account.

The second B is to BE FREE WITH WORDS OF AFFECTION. How can you be angry with a thoughtful person? A man calls his wife on the phone some afternoon and says, "Darling, I just wanted to hear your voice." He thoughtfully refrains from immediately asking, "Did you send my blue suit to the cleaners?" (She probably forgot, so he thus avoids a needless argument.) Such a husband may be amazed to discover how much happiness a phone call can bring him. And he in turn will appreciate words of tenderness from his wife in times of stress. A kind and thoughtful word spoken at the right time is like a big piece of blotting paper that can take up a great deal of discord— a word about how good dinner tasted or how neatly the broken plaster was repaired. And remembering birthdays and anniversaries is all-important. "A word fitly spoken is like apples of gold in a setting of silver" (Proverbs 25:11).

The third B is a difficult objective to attain in this day of over-organization. It is BE TOGETHER. In the first few months of marriage the husband and wife are together most of the time, but as they begin to get involved in neighborhood and community activities they find themselves going their own separate ways. Perhaps the wife plays bridge with other women and the husband bowls with a team from the plant. Both need to have recreation outside the home with friends, but they also need to set aside time to do things together. There are many inexpensive activities which couples can share, such as hiking, picnics, refinishing furniture, listening to music or singing around the piano, and reading aloud to one another. One of the practical values of going to church, aside from its spiritual impact, is the fact that it is one of the few things during the week that some married couples do together.

If you are going to promote a quarrel-free atmosphere in the home, it is important for you continually to learn more about each other, individually and collectively. Sometimes a wife will get into a mood that her husband cannot understand. He comes home from work to find that almost anything he says or does is met by an irrational hostility. Perhaps the reason is that she and a neighbor have had a falling-out, and subconsciously she is taking her anger out on her husband. Precisely when she needs his love and patience most, however, he responds to her with indignation and loss of temper with the result that the hands of their marital clock are given a turn backward. She cries out to him: "You just don't understand women." Indeed, he does not.

Women are called the "weaker sex" not because of their physical weakness, because in many ways they are able to stand up under the strains of life better than men, but because of their dependent position in regard to child-bearing. Psychiatrist Erich Fromm describes the feminine character by the qualities of "productive receptiveness, protection, realism, endurance, motherliness."[3] If more men recognized the heavy responsibilities placed on their wives, women might receive more masculine sympathy and understanding. Consider the following facts: In twenty years of marriage the typical wife can look forward to washing 850,000 dishes, ironing 11,000 shirts, mopping and vacuuming 24,000 square yards of floor, making 7,500 beds, planning and cooking 20,000 meals, cleaning the bathroom 1,500 times, and emptying enough wastebaskets to fill seven railroad boxcars.[4] How long would you stay on a job like this one when it offers the following "benefits"? (1) No chance of an increase in pay, (2) no prospects of a promotion (merely more children), and (3) no set working hours—you just work until you are finished. As Anne Morrow Lindbergh puts it:

> What a circus act we women perform every day of our lives. It puts the trapeze artist to shame. Look at us. We run a tight rope daily, balancing a

pile of books on the head. Baby-carriage, parasol, kitchen chair, still under control. Steady now![5]

The male of the species, on the other hand, is the little boy grown up. He likes to play with toys (motor boats, electric trains, automobile engines), he likes games, he is rather predictable, he tends to be somewhat of a braggart and likes to have his ego fanned, and he likes to go out in the woods to find adventure (go hunting). Fromm says masculine character consists of "penetration, guidance, activity, discipline and adventurousness." He goes on to say that in each sex the masculine and feminine characteristics are blended, but in differing proportions.[6]

An ancient sage once gave some good advice: "Know thyself!" In the area of interpersonal relations between spouses it would be good to add: "Know thy mate!"

Troubles in marriage are a reality. We know this fact only too well by the daily stream of bitter and disappointed men, women, and children coming out of the divorce courts. Marriages can and do fail. But they do not have to fail, because inner resources of the Spirit are available from God to lift each person to a higher maturity. Really all that has been said in this chapter about keeping trifles from becoming troubles can be summed up in that word "maturity." What does it mean? It is simply being "grown up" and able to cope with life in an adult way.

Maturity in marriage means having a firm sense of reality. It means being able to see clearly through the mirages, the romantic nonsense that makes you see qualities in your mate which are not there. Maturity allows you to see him for what he is and as he is. It gives you the reality of knowing that when he blows up, he may be frustrated and tired but not necessarily tired of you.

Maturity in marriage means being flexible and adaptable. Those couples who cannot change are liable to end up in the divorce court. To be mature means to give and take. A mature person is not spineless. He is what the sociologists call "inner directed." This concept is very close to Paul's concept of how the roots of religion anchor us. He says that when we "attain to the unity of the faith and of the knowledge of the Son of God, to mature manhood, to the measure of the stature of the fulness of Christ," we are kept from being mere children who are blown this way and that by every latest fad. He says we are able to speak "the truth in love" and "to grow up in every way."[7]

Maturity in marriage means getting pleasure from giving rather than from taking. When one is loved and is secure at the core of his being, he is able to give out of the overflow. This quality is part of the natural order of things given to us by God. The act of giving in love seems to renew itself even in the process of depletion. "The more one gives, the more one has to give—like milk in the breast."[8]

Maturity in marriage means being able to forgive and forget. To a Christian this power is at the very core of his experience. He has been loved, accepted, and forgiven by God, and this is his greatest gift. Because of it he can face the future fearlessly with joy and gladness and, without undue anxiety, can forgive others. Not that such action is easy from a human standpoint, but it was not easy for God either— it cost him his Son on a cross.

There are both small things and big ones which require forgiveness in marriage, ranging from sharp, cutting words said in anger all the way to infidelity. One of the most poignant portrayals of this need is given by Frederick Buechner's characters in his book *The Final Beast.* Theodore Nicolet, a young pastor whose wife was killed in an accident a year before, goes to a distant town to seek out the company of Rooney Vail, a former parishioner. Rooney is an attractive, unconventional young woman whose great sorrow is that she and her husband are childless. He also meets a colorful woman faith-healer named Lillian Flagg, a committed Christian with a flare for the exotic. She confronts Nicolet when he arrives looking for Rooney Vail and tells him what Rooney needs and what he can give her.

"Only give her what she really wants, Nicolet."

"Give her what . . .?"

". . . The only thing you have to give." And then she almost shouted at him "Forgive her for Christ's sake, little priest!"

"But she knows I forgive her."

"She doesn't know God forgives her. That's the only power you have—to tell her that. Not just that he forgives her the poor little adultery. But the faces she can't bear to look at now. The man's. Her husband's. Her own, half the time. Tell her he forgives her for being lonely and bored, for not being full of joy with a houseful of children. That's what sin really is. You know—not being full of joy. Tell her that sin is forgiven because whether she knows it or not, that's what she wants more than anything else—what all of us want. What on earth do you think you were ordained for?"

Later that night as Nicolet and Rooney are alone in Lillian Flagg's home, he does this hardest thing for him.

Then he slowly walked the great distance to where she sat and stood beside her, looking down at her profile bright against the dark panes as she gazed away from him at nothing. With his palms flat against her temples, he tipped her face to him, and she raised her own hands and pressed them against his so that each seemed to be preventing the other's escape while robed in shadow he heard himself pronounce like a stranger, "The almighty and merciful God pardon and deliver you, forgive you every face you cannot look upon with joy," and what he saw was Raggedy Ann with a mouth stitched shut in a ragged smile and the shoebutton eyes shining bright for maybe no more than a child to maul and mother her to life.[9]

A mature person in marriage is one who has found a life of joy through forgiveness and, like the father in the parable of the prodigal son, is able to forgive and forget.

And finally, maturity in marriage is the building of life on the rock of faith (Matthew 7:24-27). When you stand before the altar and dedicate yourselves to an adventure in faith, you are constructing your future on *a rock.* In Jesus' story it is with realism that he says the rains, storms, and winds of adversity will come and beat upon your house. Life is never easy. It has its sorrows as well as its joys, but with God's guidance and help your future is secure. "We are afflicted in every way, but not crushed; perplexed, but not driven to despair" (2 Corinthians 4:8).

In the inspiration of weekly worship both of you can indulge in the grace of self-examination. "Lord, is it I?" you can ask. "Am I being stubborn, or selfish, or bullheaded with my family? Am I seeking a speck in my mate's eye and overlooking the large log in my own? Am I being self-righteous with my loved one? Is my mate in better physical and mental and emotional condition because of our marriage? Do I encourage him (or her) in times of discouragement? Does my partner find in me the kind of understanding that makes outside annoyances bearable?"

Maturity is having a divine purpose for life and knowing that contentment lies in little things. It is having a justifying faith in the Almighty, who says, "My grace is sufficient for you, for my power is made perfect in weakness" (2 Corinthians 12:9).

Dietrich Bonhoeffer was one of the saints of the twentieth century. He dared to oppose Hitler and tragically died in a German concentration camp just hours before the Allies liberated it. While in prison he wrote to a friend:

> Most people have forgotten nowadays what a home can mean, though some of us have come to realize it as never before . . . it is an ordinance God has established in the world, the place where peace, quietness, love, joy, purity, continence, respect, obedience, tradition, and, to crown them all, happiness may dwell, whatever else may pass away in the world.[10]

Money buys boats and books
And tools and ties and trains—
But dollars alone are as sterile as stone
Without consecrated brains.

It takes some doing and dealing
To provide and divide the parts—
Yet humble hands can meet demands
With dedicated hearts.

When head and hands are full
With God's love for men and things—
Then luxury and lace will take their place
And all creation sings.

11
Dollars and Sense

"THE EARTH IS THE LORD'S and the fulness thereof, the world and those who dwell therein," an ancient poet has written (Psalm 24:1). On this verse rests the philosophy of the Christian stewardship of all life. God is the creator and we are his creatures. All we have and are is a gift from him—including our lives, our time, our abilities, and our money.

In a Christian home the income earned by either husband or wife is for both to use, because they are partners united in faith. However, the mere fact that they have committed themselves to God and to one another does not mean that they will not have any difficulties with the handling of money. Most of us are a long way from sainthood, and the subject of money can easily introduce an impersonal devilishness into marriage. As the apostle Paul observed, "For the love of money is the root of all evils; it is through this craving that some have wandered away from the faith . . ." (1 Timothy 6:10). Even if we manage to keep our lower natures under control, money management is still a problem because most of us have not had adequate training or practice prior to marriage. The size of your income is not as important as the attitude you have toward it. Both of you therefore will want to spend a large amount of time talking through the way you will want to handle your finances. Money may be more of a problem at the beginning of marriage than later, because (in spite of the old adage which says otherwise) two people cannot live as cheaply as one, and you will have to do a lot of figuring if you are to have any expectation of living within your income.

Probably the first thing any expert on family finance will tell you about is the value of budgeting. Without proper control, money has a way of going out faster than it comes in, and this fact spells diminishing returns both for the bank account and for the marriage. A budget is not magic, but it can be most helpful if two people will follow it faithfully. A budget is merely a plan of distribution. It works like a dam inasmuch as it holds back indiscriminate spending and allows money to be used in controlled channels as the needs arise. A budget should be a servant and not a master. If you follow yours in this spirit, it will be a considerable help to you in maintaining the stability of your marriage.

A valuable tool in budget making is a book of some kind in which you can work out your financial plan and keep a record of expenses. A ledger account book will do very well for this purpose, or perhaps you can get along nicely with a looseleaf notebook with pages about 8½ by 11 inches.

Begin at the top of the first page by writing the amount of your regular take-home pay, whether weekly, biweekly, semimonthly, or monthly. If your income varies (like that of a commission salesman or a seasonal worker), estimate a year's income and divide it by 12 or 52 to get a monthly or weekly figure.

Next, list all your fixed yearly expenses—those which *must* be paid, and which are more or less definite as to amount, such as rent, utilities, taxes, debt payments, and insurance. (Don't list any that are handled as payroll deductions, however, as these would be duplications.) Total these yearly figures and divide them by 12, 24, 26, or 52, whichever figure fits your pay period. Then subtract the resulting amount from the take-home pay to get the amount which is available for variable expenses.

Your calculation might look something like this:

Monthly take-home pay $610.00
Fixed yearly expenses:[1]
    House payments, including taxes $1,500.00
    Utilities 600.00
    Debt 265.00
    Insurance 300.00

                                        $2,665.00
Fixed monthly expenses
  (yearly divided by 12) 222.08
Available for monthly variable expenses 387.92

Now make a list of the expenses over which you have some control, and by trial and error place realistic amounts opposite each which will total the same as the figure at the end of the previous calculation (in this example, $387.92). This may include items such as allowances, food, transportation, benevolences, recreation, clothing, medical and dental, and savings, which to some extent you can increase or decrease at will. Here is how this part of the budget might look:

Allowances $20.00
Food (including milk) 90.00
Transportation 80.00
Church and other benevolences 60.00
Recreation (including vacations) 40.00
Clothing 40.00
Medical and dental 15.00
Purchase of furniture, appliances, etc. 20.00
Savings 22.92

Total variable monthly expenses $387.92

After a few months you will want to reevaluate the daily needs so as to readjust any budget item that has been incorrectly estimated. Allow money to accumulate under each category; don't spend it all in the allotted period unless you must. Don't transfer your medical excess if you have not had any sickness, because a day may come when you will need it. Lay aside some of the "recreation" money for vacation trips. Unexpended amounts should be kept in a bank account, preferably a savings account, to reduce the temptation for impulsive spending.

As the weeks and months go by, be sure to make a careful listing of *every* expenditure. Such a practice is not only imperative for maintaining your budget but also provides a mighty good record to have when income tax returns are due. Paying bills by check gives you a good record. Many families tape canceled checks to the checkbook stubs for a systematized record of payment. If you choose not to use checks, be sure to ask for receipts for your record of payment. Your budget will help prepare you at long range for the expenses which occur only a few times a year, like insurance or taxes. If you do not anticipate these, you will be in trouble. Remember that your budget is to be your servant and not your master. When starting out in marriage you will have to be experimental and plan for a monthly council together to sit down and discuss calmly the state of the family finances. The best way to have the house and furniture and other things you dream of is to save for them, and this means planning the uses for your income and then carefully sticking to the plan. It is best to attempt to follow two simple rules: First, begin your marriage by spending less than you are earning, and, second, cultivate the practice of living simply.

The following are some helpful suggestions:

1. The saving of money is a wonderful habit. It is better to save first and then spend what remains than to spend first and save anything which remains—you will find little, if any, left! If we say that we will save later when our income is larger, we are in fact deceiving ourselves, because studies show people always live up to the limit of their incomes.

2. Life insurance also is a means of saving (except term insurance), and in addition provides protection for your family in case of death. Every family should have some insurance, but too much can become a financial burden. There are many kinds of life insurance. Many policies have annuity features which mean that you are paid an income at retirement. These may or may not be good in your particular case. Ask your pastor to recommend a reliable insurance agent to help advise you.

3. Decide whether you want a joint checking account or separate ones. Many couples prefer the joint account. One family has a joint account where both have the privilege of writing checks but the wife

does all of the accounting at the end of the month because of her ability at math. One writer has commented that joint accounts are good as long as the marriage is joint.

4. Each partner should have a personal share of the budget each month to use without any accounting to the other. Allowances give a measure of independence and privacy which every marriage needs. It allows for the purchase of gifts and incidentals, even frivolous things.

5. Be discreet about buying things "on time." Be sure you know how much of your payment is going for interest charges; often it is more than you think. The same goes for loans, especially those obtained from small loan companies. It is all right to open several charge accounts, but make sure that they are paid up regularly. If you want some big item, it is usually best to plan ahead and save up for it.[2]

It would be very wise if all newlyweds waited until they had enough money to buy a house and car and all their material wants, but few do. Many get married on a shoestring. They have nothing but a willingness to venture forth, and this is not necessarily bad. However, after having lived at home with parents who provided everything, a couple of young adults suddenly on their own may need to make a major adjustment. There is a temptation for us all to want more than we can afford. To be overwhelmed by installment debts can quickly bring troubles to an otherwise happy home.

6. You will be surprised at the things you can do to economize and the fun you will have doing them. Second-hand furniture can be purchased quite reasonably and can be made to look like new with a coat of some interesting kind of paint. You can improvise bookcases with boards supported by bricks, and you can make curtains with inexpensive muslin material. You can do your washing at a nearby coin laundry and rent a freezer locker. It is far better to do without expensive appliances at first than to buy recklessly and invite financial anxiety. Also there are many ways for a thrifty homemaker to save money at home, such as gardening, sewing, canning, pressing suits, repairing fixtures, and doing one's own car washing. One wife who was highly skilled as a seamstress began doing sewing jobs for neighbors and soon built up a very profitable business in her spare time. Hobbies can also sometimes grow into sources of income.

7. Learn to shop wisely. While a wife will want to take advantage of the food specials at the markets, she should not buy low-quality food. When trying to save money in the food department, consider carefully whether the "bargain" is a real one. Plan for well-balanced diets.

8. Do not neglect routine checkups by the doctor and dentist. Such "economies" may prove fantastically expensive, perhaps even fatal, in the long run.

The buying of clothing and other goods is becoming a science today. Skillful market researchers and advertisers are constantly cultivating unnecessary wants and tastes in us as they appeal to our lower natures. Before you buy anything ask yourself two questions: First, is it what you absolutely need? And, second, is there something else more important? One decision precludes another. Maturity means the ability to put off today for something better tomorrow. There are houses, trips, and college educations all coming up which will need to be saved for. You must dedicate yourselves not to be possessed.[3]

The habits cultivated today will remain with you a lifetime. Living simply and frugally will help you resist the temptation to give your first-class loyalties to second-class things. You don't need to be a penny-pincher on all matters, of course. In fact, you should not try to save on the things which draw you together as partners, such as an occasional dinner out, a football game, or a concert (included in the budget as "recreation"). The heart of the matter is expressed by the dean of marriage counselors, Dr. Leland Foster Wood:

> The real level of living . . . is mainly an inner matter: not what the lamps cost, but what kind of books we read in their light; not how elegant the chairs, but what kind of talk we have as we sit in them.[4]

Family finance is indeed an inner matter. Money is only a medium of exchange, yet it is also a means of accomplishing our mission as Christians. It can be a servant to lift the fallen and meet human needs. This spiritual dimension of money is one of the main reasons for using it wisely.

A Christian family should carefully decide what portion of their income they will give to the work of God's mission in the world. Traditionally the tithe (one tenth) has been a starting point, but many other factors need to be taken into consideration. Paul states the New Testament principle: "On the first day of every week, each of you is to put something aside and store it up, as he may prosper" (1 Corinthians 16:2). In giving no one can say what is the right and proper amount for another. It is a matter of conscience, but it is a well-documented fact that a person's conscience can be too easily tamed. In the early years of your marriage your Christian stewardship ought to be steadily growing. It should be regular, systematic, and proportionate. To have a deep conviction that "the earth is the Lord's" means that possessions, time, and talent are ours only as gifts from God, and this principle consecrates all of the experiences of family life.

The stewardship of time is an important postscript to this chapter on money. There are so many inconsequential ways to fritter away time that a Christian family needs to plan its wise use. You will see all around you examples of what J. C. Wynn calls a "slot machine philosophy of life" where people insert a small coin with the hope that someday they will hit the jackpot. Life is too short to be wasted. Spend your time storing up the kind of treasures that will not rust or be eaten by moths. As in all phases of stewardship, discipline is required. Try to put back into life more than you have received. We do not need to be feverishly or foolishly hurrying, but we do need to have a sense of urgency about our calling. When we purposely give our best to God, we find that he gives back the inner strength necessary to sustain us. Nervous breakdowns do not result from hard, purposeful mental and physical work, but from the gnawing anxiety of worry and hatred. The key is found in the biblical injunction, "They who wait for the Lord shall renew their strength, they shall mount up with wings like eagles, they shall run and not be weary, they shall walk and not faint" (Isaiah 40:31).

Give me the will to live my days with grace,
To live and love and do all that I should.
In what I do I want it understood
That honest toil is right; it has its place.
When worldly wiles bid me to join the chase
To seek the fount of ease, as if I could;
Into the fire of toil I cast my wood
To be consumed. And God has deemed it good.

Some folks toil long, and hopeless is their plight;
Denied their due, they loll in apathy;
While others, lacking deep integrity
Receive rewards beyond their needs, not right!
The Bible says to us that God is just,
So work must be for all—lest treasures rust.

12

You Shall Labor

"SIX DAYS YOU SHALL LABOR, and do all your work," we read in Exodus 20:9. Work consumes a large portion of a family's existence. Therefore we need, every so often, to stop and ask *why* we are working. To get enough money so we can eat to get strength to go out and work to get enough money so we can eat to get strength to go out, etc., etc.? Is life an endless treadmill to nowhere? Willy Loman, just before he was fired from his job, shouted to his boss, "I put thirty-four years into this firm. Howard, and now I can't pay my insurance! You can't eat the orange and throw the peel away—a man is not a piece of fruit!"[1] When *we* come to the end of our short lives and stand in judgment before the King, will we be able to say we made a contribution to the world? Or will we feel like a piece of overripe fruit ready to be thrown meaninglessly aside?

In the past several decades we have been undergoing a revolution in the church in regard to vocation. For years one of the chief events in the life of a congregation was the decision of a young man or woman to go into "full-time Christian service," followed by his ordination into the ministry of the church. Such an occurrence is still a great occasion, but today the church has awakened to the fact that ordination to a church vocation has been too limiting. We have come to a new awareness of the words, "God so loved *the world*." Christ died not just for the church but for the world. Therefore, any true work for the furtherance of God's kingdom here on earth, not just the "religious" occupations on earth, should be thought of as a sacred task with equal status to that of the clergy. All Christians have a "calling" (Martin Luther used a German word, *beruf*). We are called to put away our anxieties and to trust God for our final destiny; we are called to participate with God in Christ through serving our fellow-men in the midst of the world. How we are to fulfill this calling depends on our particular God-given talents and the job opportunities available to us.

The really crucial moment in our lives comes when we take a stand for Christ, when we commit our lives to God and say, "I am trusting my whole future to your ability to take care of me and lead me." In the churches which practice "believers' baptism" there is a growing tendency to interpret this rite as a commitment service of ordination where the believer is ordained to the lifetime ministry of following Christ in the world. There is no reason why this interpretation cannot also be applied to confirmation.

The second major commitment in life occurs in the wedding ceremony. Here two people come together in the church to commit themselves to a lifetime of service to God and to one another. This is truly an ordination. The two persons being united in marriage are yoked in a common ministry. They are to use their "gifts" (their God-given endowments and talents) for the strengthening of one another in God's service. In marriage they are to have the privilege of sharing the creative work of God, in the bringing of new life into the world. Raising a family is one of the great joys and responsibilities of mankind. The ministry of motherhood and fatherhood is a part of a Christian's calling and should be treated as such.

In the previous chapter we cited a passage from the Bible which spoke of our growing into maturity (Ephesians 4:7, 11-16). In *The New English Bible* part of the passage is translated this way:

> And these were his gifts: some to be apostles, some prophets, some evangelists, some pastors and teachers, to equip God's people for work in his service. . . .[2]

Here is clearly stated the principle that *all* Christians are to be trained ("equipped") to share in God's unfinished work in the world.

If as Christians we are to think of all our work as Christian vocation rather than merely as a profession or job, what does this concept mean to the family?

First, it means that husband and wife are to be one in the total over-all enterprise of ministry or work for God. As a part of the church, they are to help reveal God's love for the world and his presence in it; they are to serve the world not primarily by special "religious" functions but mainly by a style of life at home, play, and work which is patterned from the life, teachings, and living Spirit of Jesus Christ.

Second, it means that they are mutually involved in making a living so as to provide the physical necessities. Simply because the wife does not go to an office, or factory, or bank every day with her husband does not mean she has nothing to do with his earning of a living. If she and her husband are one, they have a mutual responsibility toward one another. His emotional stability depends a great deal on her skillful ability to calm him when he is upset, listen to him when he dreams of the future, encourage him to launch out with new ideas, and comfort him when he meets with failure. The salary he brings home is just as much hers as it is his. In this light she should have just as much to say about the way it should be spent.[3]

In the third place, they have a mutual ministry outside of the job and the home to the world around them. Jesus prayed to God that "as thou didst send me into the world, so I have sent them into the world" (John 17:18). In the complex and stratified American society of today, a great deal of inner discipline is necessary to get beyond the little world of comfortable routine, particularly if one lives in the suburbs. We are too isolated from the poverty and pathos of the city's ghettos. When a presidential candidate in 1960 spoke of the 17,000,000 hungry and poor, most Americans pooh-poohed his words. An influential owner of a number of newspapers was a typical reactor. He said the statement could not be true because *he* did not know a single one of the silent millions. True. Most of us do not; we are totally separated from slum-dwellers and from those forgotten in public institutions. We are insulated by islands of affluent middle-class conformity, where there is a built-in lack of empathy for all but the neighbor next door. It is so easy to get caught up in the rat-race of routine—bridge clubs, bowling leagues, clubs, skiing jaunts, etc.—that we do not have any time for the important part of our "calling."

Many churches are advocating that their members should tithe their time as well as their incomes, and this challenge may well be the answer. The local church has a first claim on a portion of this time. There are calls to be made on shut-ins, visits to new people, boards and committees where counsel is needed, classes to be taught, and conferences to be attended. But there are also needs outside the church—civic agencies, political parties, United Fund drives, chambers of commerce, labor unions, civic associations, PTA's, scouting, art museums, symphony orchestras, schools—the list is endless.

Fourth, the concept of vocation has to do with the home. There is a mutual ministry here with a house to furnish and keep up, children to raise, grounds to maintain, vacations to take, and a hundred and one other details. Again the accent is upon mutuality. Counterbalancing the earning responsibility of the husband, the wife must necessarily spend more time alone working at home, but homemaking is a joint enterprise. Much of the over-all planning can be done together.

Many problems in marriage occur because the concept of vocation has not been clearly understood or well enough defined. If the husband and wife do not think of themselves as partners cooperating in a mutual ministry for God, there is a breakdown in roles. The man comes to look at the home as a convenience and his wife as a kind of servant who cooks his meals and irons his shirts.

The corruption of the idea of vocation is well illustrated by the incident of a six-year-old girl who had picked up several choice expressions she heard her parents using. One day she asked her bachelor teacher why he was not married. "You mean you don't have a wife?" "No, I don't." "Well then," she asked, "Who does your dirty work?" Apparently she had heard her mother refer to the routine chores of the home as "dirty work." Granted there is a certain monotony in the everyday repetitive tasks, but here again much depends upon the attitude of the husband. If he will share with his wife in the work and planning and will verbally support her with his encouragement, she will feel that the work she does has greater dignity and it will be infused with a deeper meaning.

A great deal has been unfairly said and written about the meaninglessness of housework. A woman's calling as mother and homemaker can be challenging and creative. Any enterprising woman with a flair for the unusual can find a gold mine of opportunities in her work. Cooking can be a science with endless possibilities. Great enjoyment can be had in trying out new recipes. Interior decorating is another unlimited field for experimentation. The raising of indoor plants is still another enterprise which has wonderful satisfactions connected with it. Much needs to be said in favor of the sacred responsibility of homemaking and motherhood.

The concept of Christian vocation is equally important to the family's breadwinner. Too many men drift into a job without any questions other than "How much does it pay?" or "Does it offer frequent promotions?" These are definitely something to think about in deciding on a job, but the idea of work as a part of one's Christian vocation should add other dimensions. Is the work I am doing needful and useful to society? Am I able to see my job as doing something constructive for the world? Am I serving my fellowmen through my labors? Almost any job you can think of has some value to contribute to the world, but some are more productive for the common good than others. And a few are definitely opposed to the general good and thus unsuitable for men called by God. Many, for instance, will feel that any connection with professional gambling or with the alcoholic beverage industry is contrary to the spirit of Christian vocation.

We need to catch something of the sacramental value of work which may take precedence over the monetary rewards and advancement of a job. The farmer whose only thought was piling up wealth so he could spend his days in selfish pleasures was called "a fool" by our Lord, who added the injunction that "he who lays up treasures for himself . . . is not rich toward God" (Luke 12:21). Numerous school teachers have passed up opportunities of advancement to higher administrative posts because of their Christian concern for face-to-face contacts with children. Many a pastor has passed up lucrative offers from larger churches and has sacrificially remained in small out-of-the-way country pastorates because of a sense of commitment to his people.

What about those individuals who drift into a job but realize years later they would like to be in some other line of more useful and productive work? Is it too late to change? Can they give up their seniority rights, the security they have obtained over the years, and perhaps a certain standard of living to start all over again? Naturally these factors cannot be dismissed lightly—but neither can the implications found in the familiar lines:

> *Only one life, 'twill soon be past;*
> *Only what's done for Christ will last.*[4]

Remember the story of Albert Schweitzer, who was over thirty years of age when he decided to change his work and study medicine.

If one does not have the courage of his convictions to make the necessary sacrifices, he will become increasingly frustrated and unhappy. A wife who shares the idea of vocation with her husband will do all she can to help him share the load. Life is too short for it to be wasted on inconsequential tasks no matter how high may be the pay. As Willy Loman prophetically says, "a man is not a piece of fruit!"[5]

Should the wife work outside the home? There are no right or wrong answers to this question, because much depends upon the circumstances. Sometimes her job is a necessity, as in helping her husband through school. Some women work during the first years of marriage in order to help purchase a house or pay off some debt. This decision usually means the postponement of children, and the decision may be good. If a wife does work, it is wise to deposit her net income (after taxes and her extra expenses) in a special savings account rather than use it for current expenses. The reason for keeping her money out of the operating budget is that spending her income has the short-term effect of raising the standard of living, and the adjustment which becomes necessary when the wife ceases to work can be very difficult.

The major problem of wives' working outside the home is focused when children arrive. The World Health Organization has disclosed that the most serious cases of mental illness have their origin in childhood neglect. It is generally understood that the most formative years in a child's life are the early ones. Although special circumstances may justify a mother's working outside the home, it often makes real sense for her to forgo outside employment once a baby arrives so that she may devote all of her energies and talents to the home.

Life demands commitment. A decision for one set of values eliminates others. When we decide for Christ and put his way first in our lives, we are putting rival faiths and philosophies out of the picture. When we commit ourselves to the idea of vocation in the Christian sense, we are placing our top valuation on the home and the raising of children. This point of view eliminates any outside pursuits which would conflict with the children's need for the care of a mother.

A great psychological change occurs in the wife when the last child leaves home. She has reached a turning-point in her life, with perhaps another quarter of a century of good years ahead. This may be the time to go back to teaching or helping a husband in business. If the family's financial circumstances have improved substantially, it may be the time to attempt those creative pursuits which time has never allowed, such as painting, writing, or travel.

To participate with Christ in serving our fellowman in the midst of the world is part of our calling. A dedicated husband and wife are part of the front-line troops who are actively engaged in our Lord's battle for the world. They are in the fight together.

The sands of time are running fast: We two
Have reached a point where rest is near,
But no, there is in life too much, my dear,
So let us reunite our faith anew.
We must repledge a love that's deep and true,
Forget the sand that fell throughout the year.
Think only of today; and if a tear
Must fall, I'll match it with my love for you.

Dear God, I thank you for this life begun,
I thank you for my sweet and loving wife.
I thank you for the good that has been done,
And yet we've had our share of hurt and strife.
This verse a pause, to note the joys we've won,
Then onward plod to make the most of life.

13
The Eternal Rhythm

THE THREE MAJOR DECISIONS facing a man and a woman as they pass through this world are (1) the choice of a life mate, (2) the choice of a life work, and (3) the choice of a life philosophy. The primary decision, that which is the keystone of the arch, is the choice of a faith. What a person believes has a great deal to do with the person he marries and the work he does. It has been the theme of this book that the Christian faith offers a family the resources which enable them to overcome their basic anxieties and give them a security to live creatively and triumphantly in a world filled with chaos. Furthermore, when properly understood, it gives them a springboard from which they can soar high into the air of God's freedom and love. It can be exhilarating and breathtaking, like a plunge into a cool lake on a hot, steamy day.

One cannot be Christian in isolation. As the earth is essential to all creatures, so is the church to all Christians. God calls each family into being, into oneness. He bids them to become his co-workers in the wondrous and exciting task of creating a Christian home. He also calls them to participate in the church, the body of Christ (Romans 12:5).

As Christian families come to a local, gathered fellowship of believers (*koinonia*) which meets for worship as a neighborhood church and participates in a hearing of God's Word and in the breaking of bread, they are inspired and strengthened to return to their homes and work to become more responsibly Christlike stewards in their family lives. Hence like breathing comes an eternal rhythm—an ingathering of God's Spirit and strength and an outpouring of living sacrifice upon the altars of the world.

It is our coming together in worship which gives meaning to our life in the world. When we come to church with an openness of mind and a sincere desire to plumb the depths of reality, we find answers. Who are we? We are sinners. We are people who are basically selfish and who seek to place ourselves at the center of things. We are people, as novelist Camus said, who are infected with the plague of pride. By ourselves we cannot love our enemies and do not know how to love our friends. We are helpless, and Paul's pathetic cry echoes our own agony: "Who will deliver me from this body of death?" (Romans 7:24). Whose are we? We are God's. What we could not do for ourselves he did for us. He sent his own Son into the world to die on a cross for us and this fact is the good news! "But now in Christ Jesus you who once were far off [in sin] have been brought near in the blood of Christ. For he is our peace. . . . So then you are no longer strangers and sojourners, but you are fellow citizens with the saints and members of the household of God" (Ephesians 2:13, 14, 19). We are God's and we are consequently set free from needless worry about our security or status. Through Christ we are accepted, loved, and forgiven. For whom are we? For our neighbor. "You shall love your neighbor as yourself" (Romans 13:9). We are debtors to God's gracious love in Christ and therefore are freed from our self-seeking to serve our fellowmen, beginning with our closest neighbor, our marriage-mate!

For many families in our day a critical problem is that of which church to attend, as the traditional denominational lines of many Protestant churches become less sharply defined. Unfortunately the standard which too many people use in choosing a church is not "How faithfully is the congregation carrying out its Christian mission?" or "Is Christ being faithfully preached and served?" but rather "Is the pastor friendly and congenial?" or "Is the building close to my home?" Many learned scholars have made biting criticisms of the churches today. They have said that never before have the churches been so affluent yet so ineffective. Some are saying that the "American way of life" is subtly supplanting the gospel and that many churches, instead of being "in and not of the world," appear to be "of but not in it." These are serious charges. If the message of the churches becomes watered down and the churches become captive of middle-class culture, they cannot fulfill their God-intended role.

In choosing a church there are two options open to a young married couple. The first is to disregard the location but search for a church where the members are taking their discipleship seriously. One good index is the percentage of a church's budget being given to causes outside itself. The second option is to pick a church and dedicate yourselves to being a leavening influence in it. Much will depend on your own experience. If you both came from an active church background and have a depth of commitment, choose the latter. If you are new to Christianity, then you may well prefer the former, where you can be inspired and helped to grow spiritually.

Whatever church you choose, you will want to be in attendance every Sunday. Most of the studies predicting the success of marriages indicate that the happiness and stability are closely linked with frequency of attendance. Another factor in predicting marital happiness is whether either or both partners attended church or church school (or both) in childhood. It's a little late for you to do anything about that element, but there is still time to give your children a good start.

Worship should be at the center of a family's experience. All other activities gain their significance from this focal point. It is in the presence of God in company with other believers that life is seen in its cosmic dimension. In the light of God's holy love we are able to see ourselves and make a conscious effort to throw off all the superficial and unworthy elements that, like barnacles, have attached themselves to us during the week. Through the Word of God as it is recorded in the Bible and interpreted in the hymns, anthems, prayers, and sermon, new life is proclaimed, and forgiveness and healing are freely offered to those who confess and repent. Worship is our response to God's mighty acts. In the biblical drama we become the actors. When Moses stood before the burning bush, God commanded him to take off his shoes because he was standing on holy ground (Exodus 3:1-5). However, Moses was expected to put his shoes back on afterward and lead his nation out of Egypt. In the mystery and awe of worship (the burning bush) we come to praise and bless God; and, like Moses, we come to get our marching orders. We come to be sent! Unless we are humble and open to God's creative mysteries we will not be able to respond. As Elizabeth Barrett Browning wrote,

> *Earth's crammed with heaven,*
> *And every common bush afire with God;*
> *But only he who sees, takes off his shoes—*
> *The rest sit round it and pluck blackberries;*
> *And daub their natural faces unaware. . . .*[1]

Worship is a Christian's spiritual food, without which he will starve. He comes from the world, he worships, and then he goes back out into the world. He gathers with others for inspiration and renewal and then goes forth for work and witness. Here is the eternal rhythm.

Having been lifted by the church's program of worship, study, and fellowship, we are sent out to become leaven and salt of the earth. We are to develop a style of life which will take its form from our common Christian experiences. Remember we do not *go to* church— we *are* the church. Dr. Gordon Cosby of the Church of the Savior in Washington, D. C., speaks of what this "style of life" means,

Anything which we do as a church and anything we do publicly . . . first of all, will grow out of an inward awareness and holiness. It is fundamental to everything which we do as Christians, that we personally develop a style of life which is recognizably Christian. This means that in our family groups, in our businesses and our government offices, when we walk in, a light goes on.

We will take with terrible seriousness the sins which plague us: gluttony, sloth, lust, avarice, envy, jealousy, and pride. We will not trifle with these things. . . . There will be a simple honesty, openness, a transparency about us. . . . We will pay our bills. When we borrow money, we will return it. When we say we will do something, we do it.

We will know something of repentance. I increasingly have the feeling that more cleansing and more healing can come to our world through repentance than any other way. . . . It is the realization of guilt before God. This is the reason our modern age does not like the word "sin." It implies personal responsibility.

We need to know something about repentance and we need to know about forgiveness. In the name of Christ we must learn to extend forgiveness even if we die in the process. We cannot be agents of God's reconciliation for the world if we can't handle forgiveness within our own home and within our own neighborhoods, and within our own community of faith.

With Christians everywhere we need to throw away the maps which we have used in the past, to know that we have capacities that we have not exercised.

We must make the decision that we will live on a crisis basis because this is the condition in which our world finds itself and this is what the love of God demands anyway.[2]

This "style of life" cannot be precisely spelled out, but it is clearly apparent wherever and whenever people are acting creatively and responsibly. When the Second Assembly of the World Council of Churches met in Evanston, Illinois, back in 1954, it was reported that countless busy theologians from all parts of the world would come into the washroom of McGaw Hall to wash their hands and then would toss the soiled paper towels into a nearby basket. When the basket was filled to overflowing, the towels became scattered around the floor. Nobody seemed to care as the disorderly condition grew worse. Then something happened. The person who told the story went into the washroom to find a man down on his hands and knees picking up the towels. It was the late great Christian leader from Japan, Toyohiko Kagawa. Here was truly the spirit of the Master!

This "style of life" does not necessarily mean a flashy or spectacular display of selfishness. Like the example of Kagawa, it most likely will take form as the humble everyday courtesies and kindnesses done toward the elevator operator at work or the trash collector at home. The fruits of the Spirit are "love, joy, peace, patience, kindness, goodness, faithfulness, gentleness, self-control" (Galatians 5:22-23).

After you have become acquainted with the people in the church of your choice through the Couples' Bible Class and its social activities, the time may have come for you to dig more deeply into its institutional life. One of the fundamental purposes of the church is found in the great commission of Jesus: "Go therefore and make disciples of all nations" (Matthew 28:19). The spreading of the good news is a task which needs to be shared by all in the church. Many world leaders have said that the greatest contribution America has made to the rest of the world has come through the Christian missionary effort.

A portion of every church's budget is designated for Christian work outside of the church. In years past the ladies have usually shouldered a major part of the studying and working for missions, through their women's societies. Vast amounts of money and the physical labors of love in the form of bandages, books, medicines, sewing, and gifts have been sent overseas to missionaries. The women's organizations are still a potent force for missions and every churchwoman should be a part of one, but missionary interest should not be limited to women. Today many churches hold a six-week Sunday evening or weekday evening study session on the church's mission. Some churches call it a school of missions. Whatever its name, you both will want to be a part.

The church's mission is worldwide in scope; it also involves the local scene. After all, the "heathen" are no more likely to be found in Malaya than on Main Street. The church has workers involved wherever people are—in the inner city, the rural areas, and the suburbs as well. God has redeemed the world and all should know about his mighty acts. You as a church member will want to take your share of the load in calling on new people. Your pastor will give you names and will help instruct you on calling techniques. "You shall be my witnesses" (Acts 1:8).

There are other valuable calling ministries such as visiting the sick and shut-in people in hospitals, nursing homes, and their own homes. Most local churches have a visitation committee which is responsible for sending cards, taking flowers, and making visits. Of all the work of the Kingdom the visiting of the sick may be the most satisfying. "I was sick and you visited me" (Matthew 25:36).

Another phase of the church's mission is offering Bible study and prayer groups to neighborhood areas. Two or three church members together with the pastor may begin to meet in a home some night to study and explore in depth the great issues of life. Doing this weekly can be a wonderful way to do evangelism by inviting some unchurched neighbor to participate. In various parts of the country these groups have gone under the names of cell groups, discovery groups, exposure groups, and koinonia groups.[3]

Your church also has responsibilities toward its broader community, particularly the inner-city area. Christians from local parishes are becoming better informed about the people around them, how they live, their problems, and their needs. As a result of becoming aware, the churches are getting involved in such problems as urban renewal, slum housing, mental health, juvenile delinquency, politics, and race relations. There will be opportunities for you to volunteer your time and talent for serving in such projects as a day-care nursery, an after-school recreation program for youth, a tutoring program for potential dropouts, or a coffee house where strangers from the streets may come in and discuss with you over a cup of coffee the implications of the Christian faith.

Many so-called Christians do not want to be reminded of their obligations of mission to the inner city. Though most of them earn their living there, they scurry off after working hours to the comfortable isolation of the suburbs. They do not seem to realize that we are living in an interrelated world and the high school dropout in the city will go to the suburb for his burglary.[4] A story is told of a man who was fond of yellow color. He wore yellow socks, a yellow tie, a yellow shirt. His bedroom was all yellow even down to having yellow sheets on his bed. One day he became ill with yellow jaundice and so his wife called the doctor. As soon as the doctor arrived he went upstairs to treat the man but quickly returned with a blank look on his face. The wife asked, "Doctor, is he all right?" "I don't know, I can't find him!" he replied. Too often, like the man in the story, we take on the color of our environment. We become lost in the crowd, and we become comfortably conforming. Many are like the fussy traveler who spent almost the entire bus trip moving her belongings, opening and shutting the window, and shifting her position. Her husband, more easily satisfied, said, "Emily, we're not going far, and the scenery will all be over before you get fixed to enjoy it." Many of us spend most of our lives getting a comfortable seat, and this is a far cry from the servant ministry of Christ.

When Nobel Prize winner Martin Luther King was first beginning his crusade for freedom in Montgomery, Alabama, he was shocked that his support did not come at first from Christians. He wrote:

> History will have to record that the greatest tragedy of this period of social transition was not the strident clamor of the bad people, but the *appalling silence of the good people.* Our generation will have to repent not only for the acts and words of the children of darkness but also for the fears and apathy of the children of light.[5]

Only as Christian families faithfully return to the source of their strength in God and in repentance seek his mercy and forgiveness, will they go out and take up a truly servant ministry. If they do not regularly avail themselves of the renewing power of a worshiping congregation, they will find themselves plucking blackberries instead of fulfilling their Christian mission in the world.

Jesus Christ calls us to follow him. He calls us to order our lives in such a way that when people meet us and come to know us they will be able to see Christ's spirit shining through us, loving and accepting them. This style of life is not something that we develop all at once. We have to work at it, and worship plays a big part. Our lives may become filled with the Holy Spirit but, as D. L. Moody used to say, "Some of it leaks out." We are not able to retain our spiritual power very long unless we become constantly refilled.

We need to learn to pray. For instance, if husband and wife pray together at night before going to sleep, the experience can be a calming benediction on the day's activities. Any hurts become absorbed in the lifting of lives to God's care. There are other periods in the day for spiritual renewing: on the commuter's train, at the desk in the office, while doing the dishes, working in the garden, or hanging out the clothes. Prayer can become a constant reminder of the presence of God in the daily rounds of life. We too soon become insensitive to the needs around us and we allow the "world to squeeze [us] into its own mold" (Romans 12:2).[6]

"God so loved the world that he gave his only son" (John 3:16). We, as members of his family, as servants of his way, are summoned to take up our crosses of love and service and follow. We have committed our lives into God's keeping; we have pledged our love and loyalty to each other; and through our life together—aided and abetted by the *koinonia* of the church—are to give ourselves joyfully to the world as an act of intelligent worship. We are to take the state of the world seriously, but not frantically. Jesus, our Lord, knew and experienced the suffering and injustice that go on, and we are to continue to carry on his ministry.

Once a little boy came running into a room holding in his hands a precious clay dish he had made. With glowing face he sped toward his parents, "Mother, Father, I am so excited. See what I made for you!" In his excitement he tripped and the dish smashed into a hundred pieces. As he cried in utter wretchedness, his father leaned over and said, "Bobby, it's all right; it doesn't matter." But his mother got down on her knees and wept as she tried to gather the fragments, saying, "Bobby, it matters, it matters terribly!"[7]

All of the shattering experiences in the world—the hatreds which shatter marriage, the loneliness which causes despair, the fear which is at the root of prejudice—all of these things matter. God himself takes these shattering experiences so seriously that he is shattered and crucified anew with us as he says, "It matters, it matters terribly!"

Our lives, therefore, must be forever spent on others, for we can do no less than our Master. The beloved gospel hymnwriter put it succinctly:

> Love so amazing, so divine,
> Demands my soul, my life, my all.[8]

When a family of a different race puts a down payment on a house next to you but the neighborhood tries to force them to leave, you have no alternative but to stand up and be counted for your belief in the fatherhood of God and the brotherhood of man.

Atticus Finch's daughter Scout was trying to keep her father from taking the case of Negro Tom Robinson, because she knew that Alabama whites would not take kindly to his accepting it. Atticus speaks:

"This case, Tom Robinson's case, is something that goes to the essence of a man's conscience—Scout, I couldn't go to church and worship God if I didn't try to help that man."[9]

Novelist Harper Lee thus gives the Christian formula for all activities: The worship of God and daily actions must be compatible with each other. Our common ministry to one another flows out of our worship. We come to church to worship; we go out to the world to witness. We gather to be instructed and strengthened; we scatter to work and be engaged in mission. Here is the eternal rhythm.

A few years ago a comfortable and very respectable woman built a house in New York City on Riverside Drive. She had it constructed so as to be a retreat from the world. She was fed up with all the problems and perplexities of mankind. She wanted nothing to do with the world except what seemed to meet her own needs.

A few blocks away from her was located the magnificent Riverside Church. The doors of this great church are always open, and thousands of youth and aged come weekly to receive comfort and help for their problems. The staff goes out to where people live and brings joy and hope. As a result over the years many lasting friendships have been renewed and bolstered, and, of course, the community has been a better place in which to live. But the woman took no part in it.

The world and its troubles are with us and will continue to be. Like the woman in our illustration we can build our little nest and ignore the rest of the world, or we can take our place in the world guided by the Christian faith which allows us to expose ourselves to the many heartaches and problems of people around us.

Two concluding scriptural postscripts:

And every one who hears these words of mine and does not do them will be like a foolish man who built his house upon the sand; and the rain fell, and the floods came, and the winds blew and beat against that house, and it fell; and great was the fall of it (Matthew 7:26-27).

Why all this stress on behaviour? Because, as I think you have realised, the present time is of the highest importance—it is time to wake up to reality. . . . The night is nearly over, the Day has almost dawned. Let us therefore fling away the things that men do in the dark, let us arm ourselves for the fight of the Day! . . . Let us be Christ's men from head to foot, and give no chances to the flesh to have its fling" (Romans 13:11-14).[10]

Divine Irony

We can try to mine meaning in money,
Or stalk sabre-toothed tigers for play;
Though we search for our selfhood, it's funny:
We find life when we give it away.

The raw-clawed say life is a jungle,
Where the motto is "Get what you can!"
But to get they forget the bad bungle,
That to please puts the squeeze on the man.

So if out of the flower flows honey,
Remember the Potter molds clay;
His hand makes the dark day seem sunny.
We find life when we give it away.

Appendix

ANTE-NUPTIAL AGREEMENT

(This is the agreement which the Roman Catholic Church asks participants in an interfaith marriage to sign.)

NON-CATHOLIC PARTY

I, the undersigned _____ of _____ not a member of the Catholic Church, desiring to contract marriage with _____ of _____, who is a member of the Catholic Church, propose to do so with the understanding that the marriage bond thus contracted can be broken only by death.

And thereupon in consideration of such marriage, I, the said_____ do hereby covenant, promise, and agree to and with the said _____ that he (she), the said _____ shall be permitted the free exercise of religion according to the Catholic faith without hindrance or adverse comment and that all the children of either sex born of such marriage shall be baptized and educated only in the faith and according to the teachings of the Roman Catholic Church, even if the said _____ shall die first.

I hereby promise that no other marriage ceremony than that by the Catholic priest shall take place.

I furthermore realize the holiness of the use of marriage according to the teaching of the Catholic Church which condemns birth control and similar abuses of marriage. I shall have due respect for the religious principles and conviction of my Catholic partner.

Witness my hand this ___ day of _____ 19___ at _____ in the County of _____ and State of _____. Signed in the presence of Rev. _____ Signature of Non-Catholic _____

CATHOLIC PARTY

I, the undersigned _____, a member of the Catholic Church, of _____ Parish, _____, wishing to contract marriage with _____, a non-Catholic, hereby solemnly promise to have all the children of either sex, born of this marriage, baptized and reared only in the Catholic Faith.

Furthermore I promise that no other marriage ceremony shall take place.

I also realize my obligation in conscience to practice my religion faithfully and prudently to endeavor by prayer, good example and the reception of the Sacraments, to induce my life partner to investigate seriously the teachings of the Catholic Church in the hope that such investigation may lead to conversion.

Witness my hand this _____ day of _____ 19___ at _____ in the County of _____ and State of _____ Signed in the presence of Rev. _____ Signature of Catholic _____

Author's comments: There are five points involved in the above agreement: 1) The wedding must be under the auspices of the Roman Catholic Church, 2) There must be no divorce, 3) The children are to be reared as Roman Catholics, 4) The Catholic partner is to practice his faith with no restrictions, and 5) the children born to the union are to be raised as Roman Catholics. Although the above agreement is not binding by law, it does place those who sign under moral commitment.

WEDDING INFORMATION

(To be filled by bride and groom together)

Full name of bride _____

Full name of groom _____

Best man _____ Number of ushers_____

Maid of honor _____ Number of bridesmaids_____

Other attendants _____

Who will give away the bride? _____

Have you secured the license? _____ If not, when? _____

Wedding date _____ Time _____ Place _____

Plan to be at the church 30 minutes before scheduled time.

Rehearsal date _____ Time _____ Place _____

Where will the reception be held? _____

Do you wish the pastor and his wife to attend the reception? _____

Name of organist _____

  Has the organist been notified? _____

  Have you discussed the music? _____

Name of florist _____

Name of photographer _____

Dates for conference with pastor:

  1. _____   3. _____

  2. _____   4. _____

Will you use one ring? _____ or two rings? _____

Address after the wedding _____

Additional comments:

A CONTEMPORARY WEDDING CEREMONY

(Modified from the Anglican Wedding Service)

Pastor: Dearly beloved, we are assembled here in the presence of God to join this man and this woman in holy marriage, which is an estate to be held in honor by all men. Let us reverently remember that God has established and sanctified marriage for the happiness and welfare of mankind. Those who enter this relationship are to cherish a mutual esteem and love; to bear with each other in sickness and health, in trouble and sorrow; to share each other's joys; in honesty and industry to provide for each other and their household; to pray for, and encourage each other to live together as heirs of the grace of life.

Let us pray: Almighty God, our Father, thy presence is the happiness of every condition of life, and thy favor sweetens every relationship. We thank thee for the assurance of thy presence and favor with these thy servants as they come to be truly joined in the honorable estate of marriage. As thou hast brought them together by thy providence, sanctify them by thy Spirit, giving them a new frame of heart for their new estate, and grant them, now in this hour of their pledge of love, and throughout their wedded life, thy divine guidance, through Jesus Christ our Lord. Amen.

Pastor (optional). Who gives this woman in marriage to this man?

Father of the Bride: I do *(or)* Her mother and I do.

Pastor (to Groom): _____, will you have this woman to be your wife, and will you live with her in all love and honor, in all duty and service, in all faith and understanding? Will you be true to her in sickness and in health, in sorrow and joy, forsaking all others as long as you both shall live?

Groom: I will.

Pastor (to Bride): _____, will you have this man to be your husband, and will you live with him in all love and honor, in all duty and service, in all faith and understanding? Will you be true to him in sickness and in health, in sorrow and in joy, forsaking all others as long as you both shall live?

Bride: I will.

Pastor (receives ring from the Best Man): This simple band is symbolic of the unbroken bond of love that these two pledge to one another. The circular form of the ring symbolizes the endless devotion which they both have for each other.

_____, as you place this ring on her finger, will you say these words after me: "With this ring I wed thee, and pledge my faith, my love, and my loyalty."

_____, as you place this ring on his finger will you say these words after me: "With this ring I accept thy devotion, and pledge my faith, my love, and my loyalty."

Pastor (asks couple to join their right hands together): The marriage vows which you have made this day are voluntary and equal, the same for the man as for the woman. Regard them not as burdens to weigh you down, but as winged hopes and promises to bear you up to a more abundant life. Remember that true love is not the passion to possess and rule, but the desire to give, and to share, and to bless. Let no secret divide, no rivalry estrange, and no difference embitter your hearts, but seek by openness, reason, and goodwill to find the spiritual key of peace. Be not elated by prosperity, nor overcome by adversity, but study to be open with one another and maintain a firm faith in God.

(An appropriate solo may be sung here.)

Pastor: And now, in the name of the Father, and of the Son, and of the Holy Spirit, I pronounce you husband and wife. Those whom God has truly joined together, no man can put asunder. May God, in whose presence these vows have been taken, make you blessed and a blessing.

Pastor: O Eternal God, creator and preserver of all mankind, the author of everlasting life, send thy blessings upon these thy servants _____ and _____, whom we bless in thy name. Give them bounteously of thy grace that they may surely keep these vows which they have made, this covenant between them. Grant that they may remain in perfect love and loyalty together and live according to thy will. And now may the Lord bless you and keep you. The Lord make his face to shine upon you. The Lord lift up his countenance upon you and grant you his peace, both now and in the wonderful days to come. Amen.

DIAGRAM A

A diagram of a typical church wedding party and their positions as the bride and groom stand before the pastor.

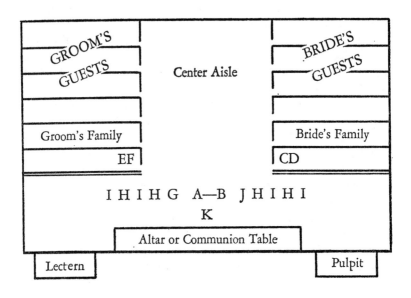

KEY:
A = Groom
B = Bride
C = Bride's Father
D = Bride's Mother
E = Groom's Mother
F = Groom's Father
G = Best Man
H = Bridesmaids
I = Ushers
J = Maid of Honor
K = Pastor

DIAGRAM B

A typical wedding reception line:

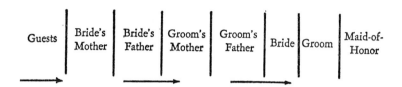

| Guests | Bride's Mother | Bride's Father | Groom's Mother | Groom's Father | Bride | Groom | Maid-of-Honor |

If you prefer, Bridesmaids can be included in line. However, you may wish them to help serve the punch or do some other chore. The spotlight is on the Bride. It is not customary for the Best Man and Ushers to be in the line. The location of the fathers in the line is variable, and even their participation here is optional.

DIAGRAM C

A possible placement of persons at a wedding dinner:

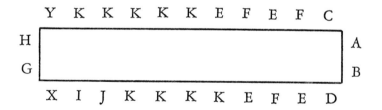

KEY:
A = Bride
B = Groom
C = Best Man
D = Maid of Honor
E = Ushers
F = Bridesmaids

G= Groom's Mother
H = Bride's Father
I = Bride's Mother
J = Groom's Father
K = Relatives and Friends
X = Pastor
Y = Pastor's Wife

Notes

PREFACE

[1] George L. Earnshaw, "My House," *The Watchman Examiner,* March 28, 1957. Used by permission.

CHAPTER 1: MIRAGES IN MARRIAGE

[1] Walter Boulton, *Marriage* (New York: The Seabury Press, Inc., and London: S.P.C.K., 1963), p. 29.

[2] Howard Moody, "The Covenant of Intimacy," *How,* Vol. 5, No. 3, July, 1963.

CHAPTER 2: THE LOOK OF LOVE

[1] Harper Lee, *To Kill a Mockingbird* (Philadelphia: J. B. Lippincott Company, 1960), p. 36. Copyright © 1960 by Harper Lee. Used by permission of J. B. Lippincott Company and William Heinemann Ltd. Publishers.

[2] Erich Fromm, *Man for Himself* (New York: Holt, Rinehart & Winston, Inc., 1947), p. 100.

[3] 1 Corinthians 13:4-8a.

[4] Quoted from the telecast Faith for Today series, *Building a Happy Home,* William and Virginia Fagal, pp. 23-24.

CHAPTER 3: OUR RELIGIOUS ROOTS

[1] Albert Camus, *The Plague* (New York: Alfred A. Knopf, 1948), p. 229.

CHAPTER 4: BACKGROUNDS ARE BASIC

[1] *Pre-Marital Counseling Guide,* Board of Youth Activities, 2445 Park Avenue, Minneapolis, Minnesota 55404.

[2] We shall mention two: *Sex Without Fear,* by S. A. Lewin and John Gilmore (New York: Medical Research Press, 1950); *Sexual Harmony in Marriage,* by Oliver M. Butterfield (New York: Emerson Books, Inc., 1953).

[3] See Appendix for a copy of "Ante-Nuptial Agreement." Since the Second Vatican Ecumenical Council, the Pope has permitted the use of oral rather than written promises. However, the content of the promise is unchanged.

[4] James A. Pike, *If You Marry Outside Your Faith* (New York: Harper & Row, Publishers, 1954), pp. 90-91.

CHAPTER 5: MATURITY MEANS DISCIPLINE

[1] Arthur Miller, *Death of a Salesman* (New York: The Viking Press, Inc., 1949), p. 130. Copyright © 1949 by Arthur Miller.

[2] Evelyn Millis Duvall, *Why Wait till Marriage?* (New York: Association Press, 1965), p. 42.

[3] Peter Bertocci, *The Human Venture in Sex, Love, and Marriage* (New York: Association Press, 1951), pp. 30-31.

[4] A wonderful treatment of sin and forgiveness is given in William Hamilton's little volume, *The Christian Man* (Philadelphia: Westminster Press, 1956).

CHAPTER 6: WEDDING BELLS

[1] Mr. Oplinger has been the organist at the First Baptist Church, Syracuse, New York, since 1934.

[2] Such a modified ceremony appears in the Appendix.

[3] An example of this is found in the following Quaker marriage vows: The couple stands in the presence of the gathered Society of Friends and says to each other the following: "In the presence of the Lord and before these friends, I, *name,* take thee, *name,* to be my wife, promising, with divine assistance, to be unto thee a loving and faithful husband (wife) so long as we both shall live." See Elton Trueblood's *The Common Ventures of Life* (New York: Harper & Row, Publishers, 1949), p. 52.

[4] Henry A. Bowman, *A Christian Interpretation of Marriage* (Philadelphia: Westminster Press, 1959), p. 41. © 1959, W. L. Jenkins. Used by permission.

[5] As quoted in *The Book of Common Prayer.*

[6] Bowman, *op. cit.,* p. 42.

[7] If the church has two or more aisles, consult the pastor for the right procedure.

[8] See Diagram B in the Appendix for a suggested plan.

[9] See Diagram C in the Appendix for a suggested seating arrangement.

CHAPTER 7: A PURPOSEFUL INTERLUDE

[1] Robert O. Blood, *Anticipating Your Marriage* (New York: The Free Press of Glencoe, Inc., 1955), p. 196. Used by permission of The Macmillan Company.

[2] F. Alexander Magoun and R. M. Magoun, *Love and Marriage* (New York: Harper & Row, Publishers, 1948), pp. 199-200.

CHAPTER 8: LIVING TOGETHER: A PARTNERSHIP OF EQUALS

[1] Robert N. Rodenmayer, *I John Take Thee Mary* (New York: The Seabury Press, 1962), p. 18.

[2] Erich Fromm, *The Art of Loving* (New York: Harper & Row, Publishers, 1956), pp. 58-59. Copyright © 1956 by Erich Fromm.

[3] For an excellent treatment of this theme seek Karl A. Menninger and J. L. Menninger, *Love Against Hate* (New York: Harcourt, Brace and Co., 1942).

[4] Lee, *op.cit.*, pp. 117-118.

[5] Lorraine Hansberry, *A Raisin in the Sun* (New York: Random House, Inc., 1959), pp. 120-121.

CHAPTER 9: THE SEXUAL SIDE OF LOVE AND MARRIAGE

[1] Rudolph Besier, *The Barretts of Wimpole Street* (Boston: Little, Brown and Company, 1930), pp. 103-105.

[2] *The Art of Loving*, p. 89.

[3] Author unknown, "Love," *Masterpieces of Religious Verse* (New York: Harper & Row, Publishers, 1948), pp. 329-330.

[4] See Theodor Bovet, *Love, Skill, and Mystery,* A Handbook to Marriage (New York: Doubleday & Co., 1958), p. 85.

[5] Floyd Martinson, *Marriage and the American Ideal* (New York: Dodd, Mead and Co., 1960), p. 340.

[6] D. R. Mace, "Are Sex Manuals a Threat to Happy Marriages?" *McCall's,* January, 1958, p. 53.

[7] Anne Morrow Lindbergh, *Gift from the Sea* (New York: Pantheon Books, 1955), pp. 74-75. Copyright 1955 by Anne Morrow Lindbergh. Reprinted by permission of Pantheon Books, a Division of Random House, Inc., and Chatto Windus Ltd.

[8] *Ibid.*, p. 108.

[9] John Rock, *The Time Has Come* (New York: Alfred A. Knopf, 1963).

[10] Lutheran Church in America, *Minutes of the Second Biennial Convention,* July 2-9, 1964, p. 494.

[11] From the Minutes of the 1962 Sessions of the Philadelphia Yearly Meeting of the Religious Society of Friends.

CHAPTER 10: TROUBLES OR TRIFLES?

[1] A paraphrasing of Phyllis McGinley's "How the War Began," *Times Three* (New York: Viking Press, 1960).

[2] Lee, *op. cit.*, p. 38.

[3] *The Art of Loving,* p. 36.

[4] I am indebted to a Mr. Robert Howard of Monrovia, Calif., for these interesting statistics, but have not the foggiest notion how he arrived at them!

[5] Lindbergh, *op. cit.,* p. 26.

[6] *The Art of Loving,* p. 36.

[7] Ephesians 4:13-16.

[8] Lindbergh, *op. cit.,* p. 47.

[9] Frederick Buechner, *The Final Beast* (New York: Atheneum Publishers, 1965), pp. 114-115, 117-118. Copyright © 1965 by Frederick Buechner. Reprinted by permission of Atheneum Publishers and Chatto and Windus Ltd.

[10] Dietrich Bonhoeffer, *Prisoner for God* (New York: The Macmillan Company, © 1953), p. 37.

CHAPTER 11: DOLLARS AND SENSE

[1] Tithers will want to include under fixed expenses the amount they are setting aside as a tithe.

[2] Interest on installment buying can run as high as 40% of the purchase price. Running up high charge-account debts has necessitated millions of American men to "moonlight" (hold a second job to help meet expenses). The frequent results of this practice—a lonely wife and a grouchy, tired husband—do not help the marriage relationship!

[3] I am indebted to M. A. and H. B. Walker for the chapter entitled, "Dollar Disciplines at Home" in their *Venture of Faith* (New York: Harper & Row, Publishers, 1959).

[4] Leland Foster Wood, *Harmony in Marriage* (Manhasset, N. Y.: Round Table Press, 1960), p. 37. Copyright by Round Table Press.

CHAPTER 12: YOU SHALL LABOR

[1] Arthur Miller, *op. cit.,* p. 85.

[2] Ephesians 4:11-12, *The New English Bible.* ©The Delegates of the Oxford University Press and The Syndics of the Cambridge University Press, 1961.

[3] Some large American corporations are recognizing the validity of a wife as an integral part of the male employee they hire. Many personnel directors interview wives with their husbands to make sure the woman is psychologically prepared to support and encourage her husband to do his job well.

[4] Author unknown.

[5] Miller, *op. cit.,* p. 85.

CHAPTER 13: THE ETERNAL RHYTHM

[1] Elizabeth Barrett Browning, "Aurora Leigh," Seventh Book, lines 821-825.

[2] Elizabeth O'Connor, *Call To Commitment* (New York: Harper & Row Publishers, 1963), pp. 160-163.

[3] See John L. Casteel, ed., *Spiritual Renewal Through Personal Groups* (New York: Association Press, 1957) ; Harold W. Freer and Francis B. Hall, *Two or Three Together* (New York: Harper & Row, Publishers, 1954) ; and Robert A. Raines, *New Life in the Church* (New York: Harper & Row, Publishers, 1961).

[4] "Last year, suburban crime rate rose 18%, an increase five per cent greater than in the cities." *Ebony* Magazine, August, 1965, Vol. 20, p. 167.

[5] Martin Luther King, Jr., *Stride Toward Freedom* (New York: Harper & Row, Publishers, 1958), p. 202 (Italics mine).

[6] *The New Testament in Modern English.* Copyright J. B. Phillips, 1958. Used by permission of The Macmillan Company and Geoffrey Bles Ltd.

[7] E. and A. M. Brown, "Christian Heritage Is Sensed, Taught, Caught," *Children's Religion,* March, 1964. Copyright by The United Church Press.

[8] Isaac Watts, "When I Survey the Wondrous Cross."

[9] Lee, *op. cit.,* p. 113.

[10] Phillips, *op. cit.*

Memoranda